You Are Not Addicted To Cigarette Smoking You Are Starving

How the Magic Mineral Prevents the Desire to Smoke

Garnet M Perry

You Are Not Addicted To Cigarette Smoking You Are Starving
Third Edition

Copyright © 2019 Garnet M Perry

All rights reserved. No part of this book may be reproduced or transmitted in any form or by any means without written permission from the author.

ISBN (978-0-9851353-6-2)

Published in USA by
Paracelsus Press an imprint of
Seven Pillars House Publishing

The information provided in this book is designed to provide helpful information on the subjects discussed. This book is not meant to be used to diagnose or treat any condition, medical or otherwise. For diagnosis of any medical problem consult your own physician. The publisher and author are not responsible for any health or allergy needs that may require medical supervision and are not liable for any damage or negative consequences from any treatment, action, application or preparation, to any person reading or following the information in this book.

Table of Contents

How to Use This Book 1

Introduction
A New Hope 3

Chapter One
The Ways of the Force 21

Chapter Two
No Escape 40

Chapter Three
Paradigm Lost 74

Chapter Four
Unveiling of a Vitamin 101

Chapter Five
The Magic Mineral 115

Chapter Six
The End of Starvation is the End of Smoking 137

Chapter Seven
Pica Solved! 184

Chapter Eight
Revelations 193

Chapter Nine
Vapers Are Starving Too 199

About 207

Soli Deo Gloria

HOW TO USE THIS BOOK

Above all else, this book is practical.

As most books do, you'll find many words and many ideas (and one big idea)— but in the end it is all just to buttress and support a practical point. This point can be summed up rather easily:

If you do step A then a thing B will happen.

In this case, *if* you follow the directions in chapter six *then* you will be rid of your smoking cravings for good. It's really that simple.

So if you don't want to wade through words which teach vital concepts you can certainly fast forward and go to chapter six right now. That is perfectly fine and understandable.

Many people have taken this short-cut because they are fed up with the literature on smoking cessation. Quite frankly, the advice or the theories in the many books and websites on this subject just doesn't hold up in the end. The theories, when applied, just don't seem to work. That means they are not practical in the least. People get discouraged.

However, in defense of the seeming prolixity of this book, I have written much for a simple reason: I have discovered the *cause* of cigarette smoking. That's what all the words are about.

To demonstrate my discovery. And it follows that if the *why* about smoking is found then the *how*, as in how to quit, will be self-evident— which means this will be the most practical book you've ever read on smoking. Why? Because it works.

Ideally, I would love for you to understand *why* you smoke but if I had to choose I would much rather you apply the *how* so that you can stop smoking without willpower or effort as soon as possible. And, again, the *how* is contained in chapter six.

I just want you to be aware that what you find in that chapter will not be like anything else you've read or heard about before.

Don't let your preconceptions stand in your way.

Read and apply the suggestions and then you will know what it's like for tobacco cravings to disappear for good.

Then you may suddenly find that you'll be interested in the why.

Share your testimony . . . along with any questions or comments.

paracelsuspress@gmail.com

INTRODUCTION: A NEW HOPE

Once upon a time I was a smoker. But I was the type of smoker that used to irk other smokers and here is why: At times I would just inexplicably stop smoking . . . for no reason. I was not trying to quit. I was, I guess you could say, an intermittent smoker with unexplained stretches of just 'quitting out of the blue'. The longest period that I smoked consistently was for about eight years. One pack every day. As you may guess, this period of smoking also ended without my trying to quit. This cycle of starting and stopping went on for many years until I finally realized what it was that was causing this phenomenon.

Of course, you can imagine why my fellow smokers were annoyed. Many of them wanted to quit smoking and I seemed to do it without even trying. According to them a smoker was not supposed to stop smoking without at least doing or going through one of the following things:

A) Hypnosis

B) Nicotine replacement therapies

C) Willpower

D) Death

I did not undertake any of these things. Whenever I stopped smoking it was simply because I didn't *feel* like smoking. Did you catch that? Sort of like after you have eaten a rather large meal . . . you don't feel like eating after that, right? But this is what was incomprehensible to my friends and family around me. The common refrain that I heard was, "What do you mean you don't *feel* like smoking?" They believed that smoking was an addiction and that it was something that was beyond their control, that it was an inherent weakness within them that made them engage in the behavior of smoking. The talk of addiction seemed silly to me, however. I thoroughly enjoyed when I was smoking and it seemed to fulfill a need. What that need was, exactly, I would not discover until years later. This book is the fruit of that discovery.

Whenever I thought of those times of spontaneous cessation a question would always pop up: *How would the psychological/medical/health establishment explain my situation*? Exactly how would they explain a person waking up one day and not wanting to smoke? No willpower involved or anything else— how would addiction theory explain it? One of the ways I thought that the experts would explain my situation was that, somehow, I was in denial. That is, I was not facing up to the fact that I was actually using *will power* to stop smoking. I knew for a fact that I was not doing that. As I said, smoking was enjoyable to me and I felt no reason to quit. Instead, what made me stop smoking was a *feeling*. Cigarettes simply became repulsive to me in smell, taste–even just thinking about them–and I couldn't figure out why.

One day I decided to put a more laser-like focus on those periods in my life where I would stop smoking for no reason. I examined them under the microscope, so to speak. When I did, a very strange and interesting pattern presented itself and began to coalesce. Every single time that I stopped smoking I realized that my eating patterns would change just prior to me quitting. Soon after my diet changed I would become uninterested in smoking. No cravings, no temptations, no nothing. Have you ever gone on a "health kick" regarding food? You know, when you start eating better or at least think you are? Well, that's what corresponded to me quitting smoking. *But my tentative theory of eating healthy in order to quit smoking didn't completely hold water.* The reason was that there were times when I knew I was eating healthy and I did not quit smoking. Why didn't the "healthy eating" work every time?

Then came the DISCOVERY. It wasn't "healthy eating" that made me stop smoking so much as it was a particular food item that I unwittingly would add to my diet. But then came an even greater DISCOVERY. This particular food item, a plant, was not the exact reason for me quitting smoking. The precise reason for me quitting was the fact that this plant was a harbor, a carrier of a particular mineral that it was very rich in.

How did I know that for sure?

Whenever I would buy the mineral as an isolated supplement and take it regularly throughout the day, it would stop my smoking cold. Within 6 or 8 hours I could not stand the smell of cigarette smoke. Naturally I shared this knowledge with anyone who was willing to listen. You can imagine the skepticism . . . that is, until they tried it. I would offer people the isolated mineral in a capsule form and they got the exact same results. Within hours the cravings would fade and in one or two days, at the most, they quit because they didn't *feel* like smoking anymore. Phrases that kept coming up from various individuals who tried this were "it's like magic" and "it's magical". Hence,

I couldn't avoid calling it the "magic mineral".

When something like this happens to someone it really feels too good to be true.

Surely, you can't just take a mineral supplement and quit smoking in one day after you've smoked for 20 years or so. That's impossible, right? Besides, wouldn't the experts already know about something like this? This sort of thinking is common when something that is considered very difficult occurs so easily and without pain.

So, a somewhat humorous backlash started occurring to me on a fairly regular basis. The best example I have is from a family member. A relative of mine had been smoking for close to 20 years, since she was 15 years old. Her husband had had it with her smoking and gave her a "deadline". They both recently had been incorporating organic foods and natural supplements into their lifestyle. While it vastly improved their health, the husband was disappointed that the "smoking habit" was still in the family through his wife, in spite of the healthy turnabout in their eating.

It seemed a bit embarrassing to him.

So he called me up because he heard from someone else in the family that I was involved in some "smoking thing". This was many years before my books and I was just testing out my theory so the "smoking thing" was just me spreading the word about my discovery to family and friends. He didn't know the details about what I was doing, nor did he want to know, but he wondered if I knew anything that would help his wife because he heard that whatever I was doing was working for people. Briefly, his attitude was dismissive of my theory but yet, in the same vein, utilitarian, because he told me "Whatever works would be fine." So I contacted his wife and gave her a short lecture about what mineral to take that would dissolve her cravings and why it worked and such. She said thank you and that she would get right to it. About a month later her husband called me up effusive with praise about my 'method' because his wife finally gave up smoking. His words still ring in my head and now I only laugh but back then I didn't.

I began to think that this was a foreshadowing of my big battle ahead *contra mundo*.

Anyway, this is what he said more or less: "I want to thank you so much for making her think that those pills gave her the power to stop smoking. That was genius I wish I had thought of that."

I wanted to defend and explain and argue that it wasn't a placebo effect— but he was too far gone.

She had just finished her bottle of the "psychological capsules" and now she would go it alone with willpower. She also talked to me a few days later and thanked me for the placebo effect of the pills because it got her motivated to quit on her own without the so-called "magic mineral". She understood now that the "magic" was all psychological. Why didn't I serve rejoinders to these people about their wrongheaded thinking? That's a book right there. In short, it's extremely difficult to get someone out of their pre-established belief system.

Maybe I wasn't too confident either though. Because at that stage I was trying every thing in my power to disprove this strange theory that was growing into fact. When I spoke to her I didn't defend my view but I just *had* to ask her about her experience while taking the mineral capsules. And she told me the answer that I expected because at that point I had heard it too many times from others. She related that "It was way too easy" and "too good to be true" and because of this, through some convoluted reasoning, she came to believe that her mind was playing tricks on her and that it was all a matter of the mind. I lost her. But I had to call her back soon because I knew it wasn't a matter of the mind and within one week she was back to smoking a pack a day. The memory of my lecture to her about this "magic"-like mineral was lost in the fog of presuppositions. A seemingly open mind now closed shut due to the thinking of the times.

I have many examples of others that did the same thing because quitting was all too frighteningly easy, according to them. Most regained their senses, however, and righted the course by taking the mineral on a regular basis. Every time that they would stop taking the mineral they would begin smoking again. Every time they would start taking it, through food and/or supplement sources, they would stop smoking immediately. The same thing happened to me many times. But I, more often, was experimenting with myself to see what outcome would appear. It really is like an on/off switch. Incorporate this mineral into your eating patterns?— smoking stops. Stop incorporating this mineral into your life?— smoking begins. It just may be that the saying, "Truth is stranger than fiction" may be accurate after all. After years of experimentation and intensive research (of which this book is the fruit of) here is the last word on smoking:

Smoking is not an addiction. The cigarette is fulfilling a nutritional demand of the body because the body is deficient in a particular nutrient. More specifically, tobacco, being a plant, supplies to the human organism a single nutrient that is deficient in the normal diet due to food refining. However, when this nutrient is supplied in the diet in natural foods and/or supplements, in which it is concentrated, a remarkable thing occurs— all desire for smoking stops.

Solving the problem of smoking is really only a matter of substitution. Substitute the nutrient that is coming from the cigarette with a form found in certain foods and/or supplements. Yes, the world has turned upside down.

In a way, this principle can be seen in nicotine replacement strategies in the form of the patch or gum etc.,. The thinking goes that if nicotine is the thing that is driving you to smoke then the patch or whatever else will supply it in a different form or mode so that you don't desire it in the form of the cigarette. One mode of transmission is substituted for another. However, nicotine is not the addictive element in cigarettes, as will be shown throughout this book. It is not the thing that keeps smokers coming back for another cigarette. What that something is will be revealed later in this book but for now I will use the term 'magic mineral'. Because when any smoker consumes a food or supplement that is rich in this mineral, the desire to smoke vanishes— like magic. Truly, it is something to behold.

To the establishment it is a foregone conclusion that the tobacco cigarette is a danger to health but the real danger here is the one that has been made in logic. Smokers are not smoking for the hundreds of chemical additives that are man-made and man-introduced to the tobacco plant. The one thing that is ignored in all the rhetoric is a simple fact: *Tobacco is a plant.* And, as a plant, it has substances that are incorporated into its very structure which, as this book shows, can be nutritive factors in human nutrition.

Again, we are not getting the full picture about tobacco.

I fully realize that there may be an oddness, an unfamiliarity about what I'm saying in this book. However, the proof will remain in the efficacy of the theory; that is, does it work? I am confident that after you read chapter six, and apply the knowledge from that chapter, that you will not only stop smoking but you will have a deeper appreciation of the big picture of why this "habit" came about in the first place. You'll understand why it is wrong to tell a smoker to quit without the right knowledge.

THE LAND OF THE PEEL EATERS

If all of this is true, society stands at a strange place in regard to how we view smoking and our attempts to stop this habit. To tell a person to stop smoking by using willpower or nicotine replacement or any method that doesn't recognize the specific nutrient deficiency, is actually an act of violence or, at the least, a form of abuse. No one in their right mind would ever dream of telling someone else to stop eating foods that contain nutrients that their body desperately needs. The smoker is castigated by the whole of society for consuming necessary nutrients. What is really happening is that the smoker is actually following the intelligence of the body.

One of the ways that the intelligence of the body displays itself is in the act of *self-selection*. This principle has been observed and demonstrated by scientists (namely Curt Richter) to occur in animals and human beings when in a state of hunger. Whenever the body is becoming near deficient, or is already in a deficient state, concerning a nutrient, a most remarkable thing occurs. The human body turns on a *switch that allows it to choose that missing nutrient from its environment . . . even if that nutrient is in a nonfood.*

It is a fascinating yet strange mechanism that needs to be

fully grasped before going further. The following parable will help us to get a footing, an introduction, into this most important concept— for it is the central principle that explains *why* we smoke.

In the following parable I am using the nutrient commonly known as vitamin C for demonstration purposes. I am using it for the sake of clarifying and exploring the specific principle of self-selection and the general principle of pica (to be discussed in chapter two). However, keep in mind that what is happening with vitamin C in the following story is exactly the same thing that is occurring here on earth with tobacco and the magic mineral.

So, as a preliminary for this parable, you should at least be aware that vitamin C is a necessary nutrient for the human body. If we are chronically deficient in this nutrient there is even the possibility of death. Before the twentieth century dawned, this deficiency was the scourge of the English Naval fleet whenever long voyages were made. Until it was discovered that limes (which contain vitamin C) prevented this affliction from occurring, English sailors were dropping like flies from the disease they called scurvy. And scurvy, we now know, is a deficiency of the nutrient vitamin C and now practically everyone knows about vitamin C and its sources.

So, you understand that vitamin C is

—necessary as a nutrient for the human body and

—you may generally know what foods this vitamin is concentrated in, e.g. citrus fruits

In light of this, imagine the following: You are transported to a parallel universe, a different world, where *you are the only person who has knowledge of the facts related above about*

vitamin C.

As you explore this unusual world you learn about some strange customs and habits. For instance, when it comes to their food, the inhabitants do something really strange with the citrus fruits which you happen to know are rich sources of vitamin C. They have discovered through their exotic science that citrus fruits can be turned into a super fuel of some sort that powers all their engines and machines (please, it's a parable). As a consequence they don't eat the fruit and it's actually never occurred to them to do so because it has always been looked at as the fuel that powers their civilization. Who would drink fuel? They feel the same repulsion towards it as we earthlings would if we were to drink gasoline.

But you, you're astonished at this waste because you know how nutritious oranges are and how vital they are as a source of vitamin C. You alone know how a deficiency of this vitamin can lead to serious life threatening disease and, as far as you can tell, there are no other rich sources of vitamin C on this planet (it's a parable). How do they get on without any source of vitamin C?

Another odd thing you notice as you walk the streets of the bustling cities of this strange world is that practically everyone smokes. Everywhere you turn, someone has a cigarette hanging out their mouth. It reminds you of the mid 20th century on earth with tobacco, when it seemed every one and their brother was smoking.

But on closer inspection you become dumbfounded. These people are not smoking tobacco. They are smoking or sucking on rolled up citrus peels!

Questions reverberate in your mind. Why would these people

suck on peels, a relative nonfood, all day, when they can have the fruit? Is the habit related to this people not having a source of vitamin C?

As these questions are tumbling about in your mind you come upon a newspaper stand and the headlines happen to be about the "Peel-eating Epidemic" which is polluting the environment (everyone 'flicks' their peels), socially impolite, and a source of health problems like bad teeth (from the acidic peel) and lung damage. The paper goes on to say that the government is about to enact strict legislation to control this phenomenon since it seems to be growing out of control.

"This is really strange," you think to yourself. "This is like the smoking problem back home."

As you mull over the odd plight of the peel eaters, lightening strikes.

"Maybe, just maybe, the reason for these people smoking or sucking on peels constantly is because they have removed the fruit for the purpose of fueling their machines. What if they start incorporating the fruit into their diets and not for fueling their engines exclusively? Would they stop sucking and smoking those ridiculous peels?"

For, after all, you are the only one that knows the body needs vitamin C and this society is throwing out the fruit, which is naturally high in vitamin C— the peel eaters may be seeking it in another mode or form which is the peel, since the peel may have *some* residue of vitamin C in it!

They are starving, in a sense, for vitamin C— for one nutrient— because of their food refining techniques— but they don't know this fact, only you do. Sure, the peels are practically a non-food item but maybe, just maybe, these people are acting on good instincts rather than instincts that are called into question by the psychologists— perhaps their bodies are directing them to engage in this behavior because their bodies are deficient in this vitamin and are desperate for it. So, you begin to befriend some of the peel-eaters and you introduce your theory. Thankfully, some of them are open minded enough to listen to your proposal:

"Peel eaters, it seems that you are being marginalized and castigated for your habit, so I propose an experiment that will do you no harm. I believe your culture is discarding, through processing techniques, a necessary nutrient out of your food supply. I propose that if you re-introduce this nutrient into your diet that *all* peel-eating and peel-smoking will cease to exist."

The peel-eaters begin to look at one another in stunned silence as someone yells, "But the experts say that we can't help this peel-eating because we have addictive personalities." You can see and hear some nods and murmurs of agreement.

Someone else yells out, "Besides there's no cure!" More nods and murmurs.

But at least some are open-minded.

"Why not listen to this outsider? What have we got to lose if he says it does us no harm?"

But another voice objects by yelling, "I'm not stickin' around for this. I know what cures my peel eating. I'm going to get hypnotized again. It works like a charm *everytime!*" Everyone laughs as they realize the absurdity of the statement. But the comment makes you begin to realize the folly of hypnotism and why it doesn't consistently work for these peel eaters. If they are really starving for vitamin C how can hypnotism stop their hunger for a vital nutrient? Is it possible that those who have success with it are actually at the same time changing their eating patterns by taking in more vitamin C in some way— who knows? These are all questions that you hope to address after you get your first willing participants.

Another peel eater yells out, "Well, I'm on the citro-patch and it seems to be working out for me!" Everyone turns to the location of the voice that just uttered this and they all behold a man rolling up his sleeve to proudly display his citro-patch. "See— I've been on it for a month now and–" But the sentence is not finished as more than one person began to note the obvious. As the man proudly displays his patch, everyone notices the rolled up cigar-sized citrus peel hanging from his mouth. Amidst guffaws and criticism the man retorts, "If you just let me finish, I would have told you that I'm not eating peels *as much* since I've been on this patch!!" This gets you thinking about why the 'patch' doesn't work on your own world, e.g., why do people crave cigarettes yet no one has a craving for the patch?

As you deliberate over how to present them with the simple solution of eating the fruit that is 'stripped out' of their diet, a man comes to the front and turns around to address the peel-eaters. He then points at you and says, "Pay no attention to this man! I've been seeing a therapist to help me with my willpower and the ability to assert myself and make decisions. And I have stopped peel eating just by learning to say NO!" The man goes on to say how the psychological profession has helped him analyze why he is weak willed and how it has helped him to become stronger willed and such.

The crowd is duly impressed with this testimony and you might as well throw in the towel with your theory but just then inspiration hits you and you decide to put your theory to the test by asking a question.

"Sir, I was just wondering— since you have successfully stopped peel eating have you noticed any change in your diet?"

At this, the man's face becomes distorted into an expression of arrogant dismissal but then, as the question sinks in, his countenance changes into one of anxiety and apprehension . . . as if one is being found out.

The man spits out, "What does my diet have to do with me stopping peel eating?"

"Just curious if anything has changed in your diet before or since you stopped peel eating for good. Just an idea I've had that's all."

The man begins to shrink a little as if he knows where you are going with your line of enquiry and, as luck would have it, just then a voice pipes up from the crowd, which you take to be the voice of the man's wife, "Oh, honey! Aren't you going to tell the stranger that special diet you started just before you quit peel eating?"

Bingo! Now the man begins looking wildly about as if looking for an escape route but you begin to plead, "Hey wait! Won't you share with us what your diet change consisted of before you quit peel eating?"

Again he repeats, "What does that have to do with anything— especially me quitting?"

And you respond: "Maybe your diet change is what made you stop gnawing the peel and continued to help you quit." The shear novelty of your idea makes the crowd wonder about the man's diet even more, so they begin to ask and to prod the man into telling them what it was exactly that he changed in his diet. But first you take a gamble and decide to expound your theory. You begin to amplify your idea: "Peel eaters, I believe that the reason you are peel eating is because you are actually receiving a nutrient from the peel. This nutrient, that is necessary for your body, has been removed from your regular food supply by refining techniques, so you are turning to the peel as an alternative source."

You feel like you have to reiterate and expand the idea to let it sink in because it is so outlandish to these poor folk: *"This nutrient is in the actual fruit which your civilization removes, or throws away, in the refining process.* So, I believe, if you start eating it since it contains the necessary nutrient, known as vitamin C on my world, you will stop peel eating. This is the only reason you are consuming a non-food, the peels, because the peels contain a residue of something you actually need, vitamin C, though not in sufficient amounts, so you must eat many peels continually to get enough of this nutrient."

You find yourself repeating the idea for effect because the concept is just too important.

The crowd begins to buzz with skepticism but almost immediately there is a shriek heard from the wife of the man that gave his testimony on willpower. Clasping her heaving chest she says, "I can't believe it! I think this man might be right! You see, my husband wasn't feeling good about his weight so, about the same time that he was seeing the psychologist to stop peel eating, he went to visit an alternative health doctor for his weight, who told him to begin eating oranges. Can you imagine that?! He was desperate to try anything because of how he was feeling, so he started eating the fruit and in a few days he just stopped eating peels!!"

At hearing this, almost everyone in the crowd becomes a

willing participant in your 'fruit' experiment. Your theory is confirmed by the results. Almost immediately, everyone begins to notice a change and soon enough the desire to 'eat a peel' becomes repulsive–the cravings are just not there–because everyone is eating the fruit which is far richer in vitamin C and also far better for them. All it took was replacing the vitamin C in their diets through a whole food form. As soon as this happened, the desire for the vitamin C in the non-food form was vanquished in each peel eater.

A SIMPLE DIETARY SOLUTION

En masse, our civilization has attacked one nutrient that the body needs desperately. By methods of refining (and dietary fads), this special nutrient, a mineral, has been removed and neglected. The 'fruit', so to speak, is being thrown out. The whole food is stripped and becomes a partial-food. A partial-food is one in which an important nutritive factor (or factors) has been removed by the food industry mechanization process.

But the body won't take this lying down. There is a wonderful and amazing "mechanism" that signals the human organism to obtain this missing nutrient in some other way. Why does the body do this? The human body has intelligence and it does this out of necessity. Because, as this book will show, the mineral is a natural anti-inflammatory and just plain necessary for brain function. The intelligence of the body is trying to mend the fracture of the missing nutrient in partial-foods by turning to a non-food which may have that singular missing element. This is the principle of *reorientation* which is described in chapter one.

In chapter two you'll see how the human organism searches and obtains this mineral by any means necessary— even to the point of turning to what are called nonfoods, like tobacco, dirt, clay, excessive sugar intake, etc.

Though the principle will be simple enough to understand, it is just one thread woven intricately into a larger much deeper idea than the mere problem of cigarette smoking. Cigarette smoking is a result of something else. The something else, the cause, is what we must look at and understand. In chapter three you will see that there is a deep connection between food refining (partial-foods) and the three dimensions of man— the physical, the psychological, and the social. It will be shown in that chapter that cigarette smoking and any other consumption of non-foods is actually a *defense* against this much larger problem of partial-food consumption which causes inflammation. Cigarette smoking is a small piece to a bigger puzzle. It is a response, a reaction to the "something" that is far greater— the food refining which removes, primarily, the magic mineral.

Chapter four and five begin the deep probe into the 'ingredients' of tobacco and by the end of chapter five you will understand what it really is that a smoker is searching for. The magic mineral is unveiled.

Chapter six is where the long sought for answer to smoking can be applied to your life in practical ways. The mystery of smoking is solved, and will be solved in your case, when you apply the knowledge from that chapter to your life. No big dietary changes or exercise programs or anything of the sort. After applying the ideas in that chapter to your lifestyle you will understand the big picture, you will understand this parable with greater depth.

Chapters seven and eight tie up the loose ends by showing how the need for this nutrient morphs into other strange habits and you'll also understand that this knowledge of the magic mineral is actually ancient, as revealed by Indian mythology.

In the great tradition of Walter Cannon and Claude Bernard, the underlying assumption of this book is that the human organism ALWAYS acts intelligently. Not only when it's healthy but also when it is diseased or acting "out of sorts". Whenever the medical/health establishment veers from this supposition they steer into muddy waters in which extrication is near impossible. But, historically, whenever the profession adheres to the principle of bodily intelligence (e.g. chapter three) there is fruitful discovery . . . and cure.

It is my conviction that it is only by aligning with these foundational tenets of physiology that the truth concerning cigarette smoking can be discovered. We must extricate our thinking from the dogmatisms that are currently held. Why? Because the dogma that is out there—nicotine addiction— has not solved the problem of cigarette smoking. If a physiological theory is not successful in explaining causes, and thereby effecting cure for a problem, it becomes merely a platitude rather than rigorous thinking.

According to the philosopher Ortega Gasset, platitudes of this type are the one thing that must be 'slaughtered' in order to discover new scientific truth. In this book, as we hunt down the 'platitudes' and tired axioms of smoking addiction, a new hope will be revealed and realized in your life.

CHAPTER 1: THE WAYS OF THE FORCE

Most of the literature on the subject of addiction is in agreement that there is an inherent weakness or defect within the addicted individual that makes him or her more susceptible to addictions than the general population. It is a disease of the psychological or even, some would say, spiritual sort. So that we could label a person "sick" or "weak" who engages in an addictive habit much the same way that we would call a person sick or weak when they have a physical illness— for neither of the two can *control* their affliction.

You may have felt or heard this sense of helplessness, for the common refrain from smokers has often been heard: "I wish I could stop smoking but I just can't fight the cravings." Some call this a weakness of the will but, as this chapter will show, nothing could be further from the truth. The cravings, the emotions a smoker feels, are misinterpreted and misdiagnosed to the detriment of all who seek help in their quest to quit smoking.

A PERCENTAGE PROBLEM

We have all heard stories about the incredible resiliency of the human spirit. There has hardly been an obstacle on earth that has not been subjugated by the will of man or woman. Yet the cylindrical role of tobacco wrapped in paper, that millions throughout the world light up every day, is able to make the strongest of wills succumb to its wiles. For those who try to quit smoking we see, almost in dramatic form, a titanic struggle between the human will and a force that compels the individual to smoke. This nameless force always seems to win; it is indomitable, crushing the strongest of wills and resolutions.

But are we not in an age in which forces are investigated and causes are sought for? The spirit of scientific inquiry is to pursue and conquer forces, to find that underlying "something" that reveals the nature of that which was previously opaque and seemingly impenetrable. When that happens, the formerly obstinate, unruly force is harnessed and *it serves us*. Our modern civilization with all its technological conveniences that surround us is due to that unrelenting desire to understand these underlying laws and principles.

But we've come a long way to get to this point. An ancient Greek priest of Zeus would never be able to understand that the electrician installing the electrical system in your house is harnessing forces, previously impervious to humans, that belonged to Zeus, the god of lightning.

Would you, a modern person, consult that ancient priest about installing 'controlled lightning' in your house or apartment? But if you did, instead of technical know-how, based on scientifically proven principles, you would undoubtedly get advice on how much oxen to sacrifice and what sort of worship to engage in. So you can imagine the reaction of this ancient priest when you tell him that you can invoke the powers of Zeus's lightning any time you want, regardless of worship or sacrifice.

Enslave the god of lightning? Impossible, says our priest. So you tell him to use his method and then you will use yours. He prays to Zeus, he worships Zeus, he sacrifices to Zeus in order to produce lightning but the poor bloke, according to our statistics, only has success about 6% of the time. Is his belief shaken? Of course not. His presupposition is too deeply engrained and he will come up with secondary explanations that will explain why Zeus was asleep the other 94% of the time.

Now it's your turn. You invite the priest of Zeus into a modern home and you tell him that you can invoke the effects of Zeus at will. And you step over to a light switch and flip it on and off over and over again— without praying or sacrificing 100 oxen.

Now, here is what is interesting. If, one day, the light doesn't turn on in your kitchen, do you cry out "The laws of electricity are false and are abolished forever!" Hopefully not. You most likely will assume that a light bulb is broken or possibly something else in the circuit may be faulty. But know this, you will question everything else before you question the laws of electricity.

Why?

A law has a special quality about it. A law seems to be all-encompassing, not bound by the conventions of time or place. It worked in Shakespeare's day and it works today. A law works in North Dakota and in Hong Kong. With scientific principles we don't get "percentage problems" like the priest of Zeus with his 6% rate of success. You'll never hear people complaining about how gravity only works on certain days of the week and only on the west coast during those days.

But what do we see when it comes to addiction theory and its success in predicting phenomena and formulating principles?— which, by the way, should be two hallmarks of science. When you look at approaches within that field and the results gotten, a curious thing begins to rear its head. Yes, you start to see this talk of "percentages"— anathema to scientific laws and principles. Nicotine replacement therapy, counseling, hypnosis and every other cessation modality all fall victim to the fact that they only work a percentage of the time. The success rates after 3 or 6 months are so poor not to mention the success rates of these modalities after one year. In fact, just like the priest who invokes the power of Zeus that works about 6% of the time, so it is with nicotine replacement therapy, which has about a 6% success rate after a one year period. (Depends on the source. Regardless of source, it is an extremely poor rate)

Thank goodness your car, microwave, television, and phone do not succumb to those percentages. There would be no buyers.

What can we conclude?

Going with a percentage approach tells us that we're in the same league as those who sacrifice to Zeus.

We *know* that the light switch will work as it usually does because there are no percentages in laws.

It follows that we must not rest until we have found that "something", the law which will help us understand the cause of smoking. This is the claim of this book, that the "something", the nameless force, which bends and breaks the human will with ease, has been discovered and it can be understood.

It operates according to principles and laws.

If we understand this force which bends the will so easily we will be able to harness this seeming fury and tame it to serve us. We will understand why we smoke and in the larger context we may begin to understand addictions in general. The coming chapters will demonstrate the *why* of smoking. Once we understand that, the *how* of quitting will be self evident and will occur with ease and without any exertion of willpower. And . . . no percentages.

IF LOVING YOU IS WRONG

According to most addiction experts, as a smoker, your emotions are the driver and the locus of your problem. They are out of control in regard to their object, tobacco, and need to be reined in. In the book *The Addictive Personality* by Craig Nakken, we are told that when dealing with an addiction, the mind or intellect is out of the loop for an addict. The mind *knows* what to do but can't do it because of *emotional pressure* or urgency. As Nakken puts it, "Emotional logic works to satisfy this urgency even if it is not in the best interest of the person." (pg.9) He states that emotional logic can be summed up in the phrase, "I want what I want and I want it now!"

In essence, as an addict, you are out of control because you have an inherent weakness, emotional logic, which overtakes your reason every time. According to Nakken, and a myriad of other so-called addiction experts, your emotions and cravings are *wrong* or, at least, misdirected because they guide you into that which is not in your *best interests.* You need help.

Most people are easily contented with the immediate cause or explanation for something. The eight ball says it was the cue ball that caused it to fall in the side pocket. What about the cause behind the cause? If we go up the chain a little way, we begin to see a different story. We see that there is a cue stick involved and we also see a person holding the cue stick.

This is called taking in the *wider context.* If we don't spread our nets wider it is possible to miss a greater reality. Addiction theorists always stop at the cue ball by never investigating or pursuing all the possibilities behind the "something" that moves the cue ball. In other words, feelings are what drive addicted people to be addicted— end of story.

But what causes those addictive feelings?

Could there be something behind the cue ball (feelings) that is causing it to do what it's doing?

In other words, there may be an ultimate cause— if we don't settle for the proximate cause. If we ignore the greater context, or the cause beyond the cause, we are engaging in *noncontextual* reasoning

And if the chain of causes, or the possibility of such a chain, is not investigated, we may get the strange result of moralizing about addictive behavior. Unfortunately, this is what's happened, an addicted person is *wrong*. If you doubt this, just try to light up a cigarette in public these days without being scowled at or even derided. Every smoker is like a Hester Prynne but with a scarlet S on them.

Sure, harming the body is wrong on the face of it but could there be a greater context, something we're missing?

Let's consider an example which does consider the greater context, a principle called *contextual reasoning*: A person gets caught robbing a bank. Guilty as charged. However, it is found that he robbed the bank because he was kidnapped and threatened at gunpoint by a gang that promised to kill him and his family if he didn't follow their commands. This additional evidence, the greater context, exculpates the individual from wrong doing. The legal system recognizes this extenuating factor called *duress* and has certain principles to guide it when dealing with these situations. In a sense, the bank robbery was *right* because it prevented a greater harm from occurring and court systems around the world recognize this attribute of the situation. It would be a cruel society that would not consider the greater context in this and many other situations. There are people that actually think this way, who mercilessly believe that the situation should be judged in isolation without regard to the underlying pressure that caused the situation.

The same species of thinking pollutes addiction theory. Many judge the isolated behavior without considering that there may be an underlying factor that is causing it. There is a cause further up the chain that may be exerting *duress*, or causality, upon the situation.

Smoking, like the bank robber cited above, seems to be a bad thing— unless we look a little closer. When we looked a little closer, at the surrounding context of the bankrobber, we found a surprising condition that we didn't expect. His action was a reaction to an underlying cause, a "something else". It would come as a shock to these isolationists (or noncontextual thinkers), people who ascribe to a foggy, unelucidated notion called addiction, that smoking may be the *right* thing to do. There may be an unseen cause that is creating a situation of duress.

For many years now, smokers have been brow beaten over their habit when their actions might just be logical. In the 1970's the psychologist J. Richard Eiser found that people addicted to substances actually *enjoyed* doing what they were doing. In his paper, *Smoking as a Subjectively Rational Choice*, he lists the different approaches that had been investigated by researchers into the causes of addiction such as social upbringing, personality type etc, and found them wanting; he instead concluded that these may not be the reason at all for smokers and their decision to smoke. He concluded from his study that smokers were making a rational choice because they *enjoyed the activity.* All these theories of addiction just mentioned and others, like social or peer pressure do not add up for, in the end, the smoker smokes because there is something to be gained *emotionally.* As Eiser puts it in another paper of his, "account must somehow be taken of the pleasure smokers derive from smoking itself."

What we have here is an interesting dichotomy. The addiction experts tell us that the emotions are wrong or misdirected while Eiser confirms what every smoker has always known about tobacco but been afraid to admit, they are *enjoyable.* Cigarette smoking is *enjoyable yet bad*; this sounds suspiciously like moralizing about sin. The dichotomy can be summed up in a phrase that has probably rebounded a billion times inside the mind of those who smoke cigarettes: "I *know* it is bad for me but I *feel* like having a cigarette."

Knowledge versus feelings and emotions.

Which one is right? It would seem that knowledge should rule the day in this case, obviously, since the experts say that harm comes of cigarette smoking.

The only rebuttal to these experts are our feelings and cravings.

The tension in this dynamic between knowledge and emotions is great but one thing that has not been given its day in court to testify, one thing that has not been examined and put under the microscope, so to speak, are the emotions in the form of cravings. Should we so easily dismiss a part of our human nature or should we at least investigate whether the emotions are trying to tell us something? Maybe our emotions, wrapped in cravings and desires, are trying to tell us a deeper, more powerful truth.

FAILURE TO COMMUNICATE

The emotions, in the form of cravings, are an *intelligent language* that are communicating information. However, the cravings are not the reality but, as in language, symbolic of something else. They are only acting as a relay station and need to be decoded. Again, the emotions in smoking addiction are not the *actuality* or *essence* of what they represent.

Think of human language.

Language is *symbolic*. We all know that the word 'dog' is different from the reality; it is just a symbol of the reality, the actual four legged creature. No one in their right mind mistakes the word for the reality. In the same way, emotions and cravings are symbolizing something other than themselves . . . they are pointers to a deeper reality.

Our misunderstanding of the *representational* nature of cravings and emotions is the reason why we have failed to grasp their meaning and importance. They are pointing to something else. The cravings in addiction are the flipside of the powerful force underneath. They are completely different in mode from the force underneath but they are in a sense the same thing. Emotions in the form of cravings contain information from the great deep; valuable information that must be decoded.

Emotions in the form of cravings are *receptacles of information that go largely unheeded because our society conditions us to see information in a strictly intellectual manner.*

Another sign that the cravings of a smoker are of an intelligent and communicative nature is *specificity*. For example, by using the word *dog*, an image comes to mind that excludes the rest of the universe— we do not think of a table or lamp or anything else when the word 'dog' is specified. The word is a place holder for a greater reality. What must be understood is that the cravings or desires that a smoker has also have this specificity. The individual desires tobacco, he or she does not desire a toothpick or an ice-cream.

If the cravings for tobacco are a source of information or knowledge that can be decoded, then we should not so easily dismiss them and instead strive to find out what they are pointing to.

What is that deeper reality and why is it communicating a rather peculiar desire for a specific substance known as tobacco?

MESSAGE DECODED

In the book *Feeling Good: The Science of Well Being*, the author Robert Cloninger cites numerous experiments where it is shown that a particular emotion has a direct correspondence to a particular brain state. He summarizes one study by Dietrich Lehmann and associates in which it was found that the electrical activity of the brain was "changing in discrete steps lasting a fraction of a second coincident with transitions between conscious thoughts" . . . and that there was a "lawful correspondence between the brain microstates and the thoughts of all subjects." (pg.242) Every thought and emotion has a synchronous physical 'micro-state' that lasts from 80 to 120 milliseconds.

What does all this mean?

For every particular emotion felt there is a particular physiological event occurring in the brain coinciding with it. As Cloninger says, "Different thoughts are strongly associated with characteristic brain microstates with predictable properties." (pg. 246)

The survey of eeg microstates on scholarpedia.com sums it

up best: "the evidence suggests that brain electric microstates qualify for basic building blocks of mentation, as candidates for conscious or non-conscious 'atoms of thought and emotion'."

An emotion or thought has a correspondence to, or is *representative* of, a physical state inside your brain.

We can glean from this that there are two realms, the emotions and thoughts, ruled by psychology, and the brain, ruled by biology. There is a correspondence between the two, they are two sides of the same coin.

But here is the interesting principle in this duality.

Either side can originate or cause emotions. This is what's important to understand.

Everyone is more familiar with one origination point over the other. For example, people readily understand that, mostly, emotions are caused by extraneous events or situations. If you hear of a close friends death or if you come face to face with a bear in the woods you first cognitively evaluate these situations. This thought process which can take seconds to register will trigger certain biological systems in your body which will result in a physical response. You may cry in the one case and run like hell in the other.

We could sum this up by saying psychology affects biology. The thoughts and representations (psychology) of an event or situation (past, present, or future) induce a physical response in your body (biology). This is what most people understand when it comes to origination of emotions.

But the reverse can also be true.

Biology can affect psychology. The brain (biology) can create an emotion or thought (psychology). The brain can be manipulated into a certain physical state which can result in an emotion. Everyone knows this. You drink a few beers and you start feeling differently. Scientists like Walter Hess wanted to take this idea a step further though. When he prodded certain areas of the brain he could induce emotions in his animal subjects. The brain consists of and is surrounded by a highly tuned environment which, if altered in a slight degree, can affect your psychology. For example, if the brain has lost oxygen in discrete amounts, this will induce emotions of a certain kind—feelings of disorientation and panic and such—that are due to a physical state of oxygen deprivation, *inside* the brain. Biology causing psychology.

Admittedly this is an extreme example but the principle, biology effecting psychological states, has an incredibly wide range of application, especially since the brain lives in a sensitive environment that can easily fall out of whack.

One example of this physical environment thrown off kilter and causing an emotional state comes from Dr. Batmanghelidj in his remarkable book, *Your Body's Many Cries for Water*. He demonstrates that water-intake deficiency can effect a 'panic mode' in the individual. According to Batmanghelidj all anxiety attacks and feelings of panic are due to the *physical status* of the brain having a water shortage. He treated this emotional disorder in thousands of people through his work just by simply pointing out that they were dehydrated in a non-clinical, yet still serious, way. After increasing their water intake the feelings disappeared instantly. Once again this is biology effecting an emotional state.

Are there other elements in brain function that can throw off the finely tuned environment of the brain?

Other than water, the biggest constituent of our cells are

proteins. And proteins are made of amino acids and amino acids happen to be fundamental in neurotransmission because they are components of neurotransmitters— or some, like glutamine, are ready-made neurotransmitters.

What's fascinating is that there are many studies which show a direct correlation between our amino acid intake and our emotional status. For example, it has been shown that there is an inverse relationship between tryptophan consumption and emotional complaints. The more tryptophan is consumed the less emotional complaints while diets that are deficient in tryptophan seem to have a correlation with depression. (*Psychodietetics,* E. Cheraskin 1976) Carnitine (made from lysine and methionine) deficiency has also been implicated in depression (*Journal of Psychiatric research* 2014 Jun;53:30-7).

We'll explore this phenomenon in greater depth in the coming chapters but it is sufficient to say for now that, in the scientific literature, there are countless studies which demonstrate that deficiency states concerning amino acids, certain minerals, and certain vitamins, can all lead to an emotional outcome. Again, biology effecting a psychological response.

What this tells us in broad outline is that the physical environment of our brains has a good deal to do with our emotions.

And this physical environment can be affected by deficiency for certain nutrients.

But that's not all.

In the first half of the 20th century a few scientists discovered that a deficiency status for a nutrient can result in cravings or feelings that manifest themselves in a rather strange reaction/

This strange reaction holds the key to the solution of cigarette smoking once and for all.

REORIENTATION DAY

Deprivation of an element that is part of the environment of the brain can upset the fine balance of that environment.

But the human body responds to this upset in a rather fascinating way.

The scientist Curtis Richter, in the first half of the 20th century, discovered an amazing strategy that a biological organism will undertake to restore that imbalanced environment of the brain deprived of a specific nutrient.

In a deficiency state the organism will *reorient* itself to obtain that missing nutrient in *nonfood* forms.

In other words, a deficiency state of a nutrient causes cravings for that nutrient which, if not satisfied by means of regular diet, will trigger a mechanism in the organism which will allow it to select a nonfood that carries the missing nutrient.

Let's see how he came upon this amazing phenomenon.

One of Richter's experiments involved depriving laboratory rats of B complex vitamins. The details of this particular experiment were originally published in *The American Journal of Physiology*, Vol. 143, no.3 March 1945. When Richter deprived the rats of B complex in their food supply they all turned to a nonfood. They ate feces from healthy rats that were supplied to them in their cages by Richter and co-workers. According to Richter, "The results of these self-selection experiments on coprophagy showed that rats on a vitamin B deficient diet ate large amounts of feces freshly collected from normal rats."

Why would they choose this nonfood? "That the feces contain vitamin B we know from the observations made by numerous workers . . ."

The feces contained the vitamin B that was missing in their

diet!

In other words, even though the rats were given plenty of food to eat, they chose the nonfood (the feces) in greater amounts because the nonfood contained the B complex vitamins that they were deprived of in their regular food.

A physiological 'switch', so to speak, was turned on to obtain a nutrient even though it was in a nonfood form.

Another scientist, Leslie Harris, also discovered the same phenomenon. He published his findings in the *Proceedings of the Royal Society of London*, Series B, (Vol. 113, No. 781- Jun. 1, 1933, pp. 161-190):

1) Harris systematically made rats deficient in one vitamin family (B complex) by removing every trace of it from foods that the rats were eating.

2) Harris, at some point after establishing the deficiency, reintroduced the B vitamins in one food source only (which the rats previously, under normal conditions, always hated and wouldn't touch). The other foods, which the rats were more amenable to, did not contain any trace of B vitamin. Here was the astounding result:

The rats always eventually chose and ate the food that contained the B vitamins they were deficient in. But this was the food source that the rats previously hated and wouldn't even touch. As Harris put it, the rat "comes to exhibit a special preference for a diet which under normal circumstances would possess no special attraction for him." (pg. 181 of the volume) Of course, Harris was puzzled by this because he tried to confuse the rats by increasing the sample size of various foods to choose from. Would they pick the right food— the food that contained that which they were deficient in? Invariably, they always did, and this made him ask "Has the animal some means, as by taste or smell, of recognizing the vitamin per se? If so it would imply an ability to detect a constituent amounting to no more than perhaps 1 part in a million of the food."

Harris observed that the rats did not immediately eat the food that contained the B vitamins they were deficient in. They sampled the different foods and then when they found what worked, the food that had the B vitamins,— they stuck to that particular food and ignored the rest.

So, to Harris, it was obvious what was going on. Once the rats discovered the food with the B vitamins they recognized that that food was *working* for them in a physiological sense. Harris stated that he had, "obtained good evidence that the behaviour of the animal is due not so to instinct as to experience, i.e, of the beneficial effect produced by a particular food stuff." They ate the thing they previously hated because now it was their only source of B vitamins.

Every smoker has experienced this. Remember your first cigarette? How did it taste? Not that good I'm sure (unless you were already adjusted to it in a heavy smoking environment). It was not your preferred choice but once you puffed that first puff something hooked you. This is what the modern world calls addiction. This book will show that it is not addiction but, rather, specific hunger.

But right now you might be thinking, 'Wait, tobacco has a nutrient that I'm deficient in?'

Nonfoods can carry some nutrients. Dirt is a nonfood. Yet you would be surprised at the mineral content of some clays. Minerals that the body can use. And, as will be shown in the next chapter, dirt and various clays have been, and still are, eaten by many people.

You would also be surprised to find out how many nutrients there are in the tobacco plant. According to the textbook *The Chemical Components of Tobacco,* there are many minerals like magnesium, potassium, zinc, and copper that are in tobacco smoke. Not to mention amino acids like glutamate or even vitamins like riboflavin, thiamine and biotin. We overlook this facet because we're often told of the bad chemicals in tobacco, which it has plenty of.

In general, what I'm saying is that the principle of *reorientation* is an emergency measure that the body undertakes to correct a situation of specific hunger. It is called specific hunger because as the preceeding examples showed, the hunger is for a single nutrient. Think of deprivation of food for weeks on end. What would you do? The body will 'switch' your taste mechanism so that you'll look at things that were not ordinarily considered food in your daily life, as food. This can't be denied. There are too many documentations of this, one of which I'll give below. Now, specific hunger is no different except for the fact it is only for one nutrient. When this deprivation is prolonged there will be unusual behavior in the human organism. There will be a 'switch' turned on that will reorient the taste mechanism in order to obtain that missing nutrient in anything it can— even a nonfood.

This is what is happening with a smoker. He or she has suffered long term deprivation of an important nutrient or nutrients. This turns on the mechanism of reorientation which results in the obtaining of the missing nutrient(s) by means of the tobacco plant— a nonfood.

But if the deprivation is corrected by food or supplements

that are rich in the missing nutrient, the reorientation will disappear. The smoking will stop.

NO SIN— ONLY A DEFICIENCY

The cravings for cigarettes are looked at as irrational and smokers are told they are abnormal. But in the case of extreme hunger the human organism will override things like a taste mechanism in order to obtain a nutrient. This is the greater context that must be grasped.

The *addiction model* imposes a paradigm of helplessness. The smoker can not help his *sin*, his addiction. It is an inherent weakness that he or she can not help, much less think about curing it.

The *special hunger or specific starvation* model empowers the individual because, first of all, the individual can recognize for the first time that they do not have an inherent weakness only a nutrient deficiency. Secondly, once the problem is understood there is potential for a remarkable thing to occur.

Extreme hunger, general or specific, will drive you to seeek out nutrients in any form. Picture the scene, in late 1971, of the stranded Uruguayan airplane passengers in the desolate Andes mountains. Because of the brunt force of the human organism's demands for nutrients, the surviving passengers acted in a way that they would never in their lives have imagined. In desperation they fed off of the dead bodies from the crash. Their actions seem repulsive to the well-fed but the cell's demands are that great in extreme starvation and it will reorient the organism in order to get what it needs— in any way possible.

What would have cured them of their reorientation? The answer is obvious: Food.

Pay attention: No amount of counseling or psychology or

will-power or hypnotism or NLP techniques would have helped those starving people to turn them away from their strange habit of cannibalism. Wouldn't it seem criminal to offer counseling services for these people when they really needed food?

This is what society does with smokers. They are bludgeoned over the head to infinity with the idea that they are at fault for their strange habit, when in fact they are starving— for one nutrient. The smoker's cravings are correct and they should be recognized for what they are— signs of special hunger. Specific hunger is as extreme as general hunger.

But what specific nutrient, exactly, is the smoker hungering for? Actually, it is not only the smoker that is deprived of this nutrient. As we shall see in chapter two, the whole world is seeking after this nutrient by engaging in reorientation of some kind. This is how great and important this nutrient is. I call it the 'magic mineral' because, as I said, a remarkable thing can occur when this mineral is replenished in the smoker's diet through food and/or supplements— the desire to smoke vanishes.

CHAPTER 2: NO ESCAPE

No one has ever quit smoking without a corresponding change in their diet. All smokers who try to quit have noticed this but attribute the dietary change to boredom or nerves— the common wisdom is that it just goes with the territory.

No such thing, however.

As shown in the last chapter, there is a distinct reason for the diet change. In cases of dietary deficiency a biological organism has a built in mechanism to self-select nonfood sources in cases of special hunger. This is precisely what is happening with smokers. They obtain a missing dietary nutrient—the magic mineral— from the nonfood source of tobacco. And when a smoker quits smoking, what is really happening is that they are obtaining another source of this nutrient— which may or may not be a healthy source.

A smoker who successfully quits is really just trading one source for another. Yet people who've quit smoking successfully will attribute their cessation to various things and methods like willpower, hypnosis, nicotine replacement, 'easy' methods and such, while not noticing the change in diet. As this chapter will show, if this mineral is nonexistent or barely existent in the normal diet, the human organism will seek out this mineral in the environment in some nonfood form— the variety of which is almost endless as we shall see. And if the organism cannot obtain the magic mineral from the nonfood form known as tobacco for whatever reason (due to geography, poverty or cultural pressure as we see today), then the organism will choose another source. This law is ineluctable. Much like gravity, there's no escaping it.

SMOKING IS PICA

The phenomenon of consuming nonfoods has been observed and documented for centuries. The Byzantine physician in the 6th century by the name of Aetius of Amida used a Latin word that best described the principle of reorientation to him and that was, *pica*— which is the Latin word for the bird Magpie. Why name a disorder like this after the Magpie? As related by Marcia Cooper in her book on this disorder, *Pica: A Historical Survey*, one of the traits of the Magpie is its incessant *search* for food by flitting from tree to tree "picking up a diversity of things to satisfy hunger". Many of the things picked up by the bird seemed to be nonfood items. So the name of the bird came to characterize a behavior which has been observed in humans from time immemorial— the habitual eating or consumption of nonfoods.

In case your wondering about how tobacco is considered a nonfood when we actually smoke it: Historically, the phenomenon of pica has had a broader definition to include any route of ingestion of a nonfood. For example, in the compendium by Abraham Rees known as *The Universal Dictionary of Arts, Sciences, and Literature* (1819 Volume Twenty Seven– found under the letter *p* for pica) there is documentation of a doctor from Germany who considered "inordinate snufftaking" to be a form of pica. What the doctor was referring to–snuff taking–was the snorting of tobacco powder through the nose. Pica can be extended to include all "inordinate" consumption of nonfoods, whether eaten, inhaled, snorted and even injected. Tobacco smoke is not insubstantial. A portion of tobacco smoke is in very small discrete pieces of matter known as particulates. Yes, it is possible for nutrients as well as harmful substances to enter the body by the route of smoking.

In this chapter we'll expand on the idea of the first chapter, that the body is acting intelligently, to mend a fracture in the food supply, when it consumes any nonfood, even tobacco. The following law is due to the uniqueness and indispensable nature of the magic mineral in brain function (which will become quite clear by chapter five):

If partial-foods (magic mineral removed) are consumed on a regular basis, the body will seek to fix this problem by trying to obtain the missing nutrient (magic mineral) in nonfood forms.

The essence of cigarette smoking is the problem of pica, and the problem of pica is really all about the nonavailability of the magical mineral in the diet. Once again, the great news is that if this nutrient is returned to the diet through food and/or supplement form, in the right amounts, the pica problem will disappear, the smoking issue will be a nonissue.

The nonsmokers in the world point fingers at smokers and their 'bad habit' when, in fact, they too are likely to be engaged in the consumption of a nonfood (which acts as a carrier for the magic mineral) that is far worse in its effects than tobacco smoking— while not even realizing that the dangerous nonfood they are consuming is preventing them from smoking. In other words, much of the world is doing the same thing that the smoker is doing—consuming a nonfood to obtain the magic mineral–yet they fall under no condemnation from society because their nonfood has become 'acceptable'.

EVERYONE SEARCHES FOR IT

Sera Young has done research on ethnic peoples around the world who engage in this behavior— a 'nutritional anthropologist' who has studied pica worldwide. In her book, *Craving Earth*, she tells of an instance when she encountered this phenomenon. When she was on the island of Pemba, off the coast of East Africa, she was somewhat taken aback by the reply of one of the young pregnant women to her question. Young was wondering what she ate while she was pregnant and the woman responded, "Every day, twice a day, I take a chunk of earth from this wall and, well, I eat it." To further inquiries as to why the woman engaged in the act, all Young got was a shrug of the shoulders— 'I don't know. I really don't know. I just do it.' (pg.13 from the Preface)

Joel Wallach, in his book *Rare Earths* mentions the 18th century physician Agustus Mergiletus who wrote his doctoral thesis on this condition and noted instances of the same thing happening with women who were 'addicted' to eating mud and mortar taken from walls. His thesis is a virtual compendium of these habits. Men who ate leather, girls eating their own hair and the threading from their clothes (cotton) and women who even resorted to eating human flesh. But the disorder wasn't limited to humans. He also recorded this phenomenon in animals as in cats that would eat wood ash and horses chewing on hitching rails. Even Wallach, a veterinarian, observed at one time, "a hundred pregnant sheep in Montana lined up along an embankment eating clay." In reviewing the literature, Wallach lists the substances that are the object of this strange disorder: Paper, metallic gum wrappers, ice, dirt, coal, clay, chalk, starch, baking powder, pebbles, wood, leather, paint, chimney soot, hair, and cloth. Surely, this variety of substances compels one to give up on finding some kind of unifying property or element that might be satisfying a need in all sufferers of pica. But the fact is that all pica, including cigarette smoking, is the search for one, and only one, nutrient— the magical mineral.

We see that this disorder of pica ranges in time, historically, and as Sera Young discovered, in space, geographically. She notes in her book the diversity of objects of pica throughout the world, "Mama Sharifa eats earthen chunks from the wall of her outdoor kitchen in Zanzibar, while in Washington, D.C., Pat crunches through a ten pound bag of ice from Seven Eleven every day. In New Delhi, Simran starts her morning every day with a handful of uncooked rice . . . in Guatemala, Carlita nibbles on little blocks of clay . . . while in California, DeAngela buys ten boxes of chalkboard chalk for snacking whenever she can get to a Walmart."(pg.3)

Yes, we may feel repulsion at some of these proclivities but this repulsion also occurs, initially, to anyone whose physiology has been reoriented. People who engage in pica, typically, do not have a pleasant first experience with the clay or dirt or whatever was the object of their pica. Whoever thought that their first cigarette was enjoyable? Practically no one. But something keeps the individual coming back which countermands the repulsion of the taste mechanism. That something is the hunger of the cell because it has reoriented the physiology of the organism— for the cell must feed and find the magical mineral and if it is not available in the normal food supply it will seek out *abnormal* sources which happen to be in these pica objects. The human organism will search for anything that may carry this unique nutrient.

Can one nutrient explain the cravings for diverse items such as clay and ice cubes and chalk and tobacco, etc.?

The astounding answer is that all pica, which everyone suffers from as we'll see, is due to a need for the magic mineral.

Behold, pica in its various forms . . .

ON THE (CLAY) TRAIL OF THE MISSING NUTRIENT

If cigarettes are not available (due to geography or poverty) or if the culture frowns upon such a habit, the body will choose (reorientation) other sources in the environment for this important mineral. Clay eating was widespread in the 19th century South as Robert Twyman reports in his article for the Journal of Southern History, *The Clay Eater A New Look At an Old Enigma.* He cites various authorities and eyewitnesses who observed this phenomenon that was not only prevalent amongst slaves but also a problem with poor whites in various regions of the South. In one instance it was reported as early as 1709 in the Carolinas amongst white settlers. But the more interesting aspect of Twyman's article is his selection of quotes he garnered from various researchers who looked into the matter in the South.

A predominant portion of the clay eaters were found to be pregnant women. Comments that were commonly heard from women were, "You have to eat clay when you are carrying your baby or it won't be born right." This and other comments that the women made give the impression that there seemed to be a common undercurrent of belief, in this subculture of clay eaters, that the clay had some nutritive value. But even more astounding is the attachment and the intense cravings that the clay eaters had for clay: "I feel awful, just about crazy when I can't get clay," said one woman. Sound familiar to anyone who tries to quit smoking? The researchers found this craving to be a common refrain of the clay eaters. Now, Twyman was not writing about addictions but he weighed the evidence and came to an interesting conclusion/observation. He wrote that, much like tobacco, eating clay, "brings a feeling of relaxation and oral gratification from the pleasure of chewing . . . *once the desire is created, the habit is soon fixed,* a fact reported by the earliest recorders of clay eating as well as by modern researchers." (italics mine) Tobacco smoking begins in this very way with an initial repulsion by the taste of the substance but then a curious thing happens— as Twyman says, the habit is soon fixed. The reason why any pica habit, whether smoking or clay eating, becomes "fixed" is because of the need for one nutrient, the magic mineral.

The anthropologists Dickens and Ford found that clay eating carried on into the 20th century when they surveyed 207 Mississippi school children in the early 1940s. Through a rather sophisticated survey they found that 25% of the children had recently eaten clay but both authors felt this figure could have been much higher if they asked if the children had *ever* eaten dirt. They describe the breadth and depth of this phenomenon in their paper entitled *Geophagy Among Mississippi Negro School Children:* ". . . dirt is carried long distances to people who can no longer get it themselves. Some claim that Negroes in the South send bags of dirt to Negroes who have migrated north. Negroes who now live in the Yazoo-Mississippi Delta are said to ask Negroes who live in the hills of Mississippi to send a bag of "good dirt."

Perhaps they acquired the habit when they, too, lived in the hills where clay was abundant. The dirt in the Delta is "no good" for eating. This hearsay and personally obtained evidence gave support to the notion that dirt eating is indeed a fact and rather widespread among the population here."

Even the popular press has reported on this. *Time* magazine in an article from July 28, 1967, reports on African-Americans who migrated from the South: "Those who migrate North sometimes receive packages of clay (known as "Mississippi Mud" in Los Angeles) mailed by friends back home."

The clay is known and referred to by a nickname as far as Los Angeles? This draws a picture of an extensive network of distribution. If we add in the physiological responses of the individuals who were 'clay addicted', we have a picture that seems no different than the 'need' for tobacco and its extensive distribution today.

Sera Young references several authorities throughout history who noticed the fixation for clay rivaled the desire for alcohol or tobacco putting them on an equal basis. Note, also, the following geographical locations:

Jamaica in 1788: "Their attachment to earth is greater than even that of dram drinkers to their pernicious liquor" (J. Hunter *Observations on the diseases of the army in Jamaica* 1788)

Georgia 1840: "From the oldest to little children, they are as much addicted to the eating of clay as some communities are to the use of tobacco and snuff" (E.P. Burke *Pleasure and pain, reminiscences of Georgia in the 1840's* 1871)

England in 1842: "Powerfully do the morbid appetites enslave a large portion of mankind– from the opium of China to the tobacco of Virginia, and from the beer of England and the whiskey of Ireland to the clay of Carolina" (J.S. Buckingham *The Slave States of America* vol 1 1842)

India in 1906: "The uncontrollable craving for this earth is like the opium or alcohol habit, and the ravenous symptoms and anxiety in the faces and actions of the eaters are similar to those found in the devotees of one or the other of these vices" (D. Hooper and H. Mann *Memoirs of the the Asiatic Society of Bengal* 1906)

In Pemba, where Young did some of the research, the same word is used for addiction to cigarettes and other substances as that used for pica. It was so widespread in Laos that at one time authorities threatened arrest to any who engaged in geophagy (dirt-eating).

You could almost substitute the word 'tobacco' when these writers reference 'clay' and 'earth'. The cravings and addiction is on the same level.

Why? They both share a nutrient in common that humans need. But it is not only clay and tobacco that have the magic mineral in common. The range of nonfood items that contain the magic mineral is breathtaking as we shall now see.

LIKE TAKING DOPE

That same article from Time magazine, published July 28, 1967, reports the following concerning pica: ""When I'm pregnant, it's just like taking dope," said the woman bearing her ninth child at the District of Columbia General Hospital in Washington. "I can hardly wait to get home so I can get some more starch," she added, referring not to starchy foods but to laundry starch. "Sometimes I'll eat two or three boxes a day.""

Surely, this woman's experience is anomalous and not representative of the general population in any way, right? But the article goes on to say that "Northern doctors have lately discovered that eating laundry starch is all the rage among Negro women—especially pregnant women—in many Northern-city slums. At D.C. General Hospital, Chief Obstetrician Dr. Earnest Lowe estimates that up to one-fourth of his patients are starch addicts. At Los Angeles County Hospital, three or four patients a week are diagnosed as having anemia apparently caused by starch binges."

The theory at the time was that the clay eaters, who were largely from the South, had substituted one form of pica for another when they moved up North. Says the article in *Time*, "According to the few doctors who have studied the subject, the craving for laundry starch is an offshoot of the clay-eating habit still prevalent among some Southern Negroes."

What was not, and still is not explained, is why these former clay eaters chose laundry starch. Is there some type of connection between laundry starch and clay? At the outset it seems like there could not be two objects that are further apart in composition than laundry starch and clay. But the reason the former Southerners were going to the laundry starch is that they had no access to clay and their physiology was reoriented to choose another item in their immediate environment that did contain the magical mineral— the laundry starch. There is *indeed* a very intimate connection between laundry starch and clay as pica substances . . . and even tobacco.

All objects of pica have a unifying principle and that is that they are carriers of the magic mineral. And somehow, someway, the human organism is able to search out and find it; depending on the environmental surroundings the individual is in, whether it is in clay or laundry starch or tobacco or whatever, this mineral fulfills the deep need and cravings of the cell that starves for it. It follows that the answer to any problem of pica— whether you smoke tobacco, eat clay or crunch on ice incessantly— is to replace the magic mineral in your diet through certain foods and/or supplements in which it is concentrated. Which means that the pica disorder known as cigarette smoking will completely cease— cravings and all.

PRESCRIPTIONS FROM THE PAST

Historically, many observers who failed to understand pica had their own theories as to causes and they ranged from insanity to hookworm infestation to low level of IQ/retardation to, as Twyman reports, the accusation by land owners that the slaves wanted to get sick so that they could escape work. All of these were found wanting to some degree or other.

Because of the ignorance of the cause, of course, we can only expect the cures to be unenlightened. The 10th centurty Persian philosopher Avicenna recommended imprisonment. The 19th century Southern landowners were not too far away from that idea also, as Twyman relates, "In desperation, planters attempted to effect cures by confining the afflicted slaves in stocks, by attaching metallic masks or mouthpieces to them, and by other preventive measures to break the habit; but once the physical restraint was removed the "patient" invariably returned to his old ways."

Against this way of thinking that treats pica as something done willfully there does seem to be another stream of thought that has a long tradition attached to it that sees pica as a disorder that can be treated nutritionally. Aetius of Amida wrote that those who "crave for sand, oyster shells and wood ashes", could be cured by eating *certain kinds of food*. Though he generalizes with the first two items of his prescription, he is still rather precise in recommending, "fruits, green vegetables, pigs feet, fresh fish and old tawny fragrant wine."(pg.5, *Pica*, Marcia Cooper)

There is a prescription from the 11th century that comes from a famous midwife, Trotula of Salerno, who actually wrote a text on common sicknesses of women. She writes, "But if she should seek to have potter's earth or chalk or coals, let beans cooked with sugar be given to her."(pg.102, *Womens Lives in Medieval Europe*, Emilie Amt) So, we notice two things from these examples:

1) the prescription is food

2) the prescription of food has some precision

The inference can be taken from these writers of the past that there is something missing in the diet of the individual who is suffering from pica. There is the sense that, because of the precision in the foods prescribed, there may be a certain factor in those foods that the pica sufferer is deficient in. Because in the 17th century we come upon the physician Boezo who recommends, "one and one half scruples of iron dross taken for many days as wonderfully beneficial for men and women."(pg.10, *Pica*, Marcia Cooper) Boezo is saying it is a specific element that is deficient in the diet of the pica sufferer. Though iron is not the magical mineral, it does have somewhat of a residue of it (chapter seven) which is why it has been touted as a treatment in pica even by modern doctors.

This idea of Boezo, of pica due to iron deficiency, was taken up by modern researchers in treating pica as we see in *The Journal of Pediatrics* in an article published in October, 1964, entitled *The Value of Iron Therapy in Pica*. The physicians, McDonald and Marshall, treated children, whose pica object was sand, with intra-muscular iron injections. They wrote that, "Three to four months later nearly all of those given iron had lost their pica." The authors of the paper went on to conclude that, "Our experience is that pica can be cured by iron in nearly all cases."

But the key word here is 'nearly'. Remember that little principle of the 'problem of percentages' from the first chapter? Iron did not work in all cases simply because it is not the magic mineral. But why did it seem to work in some cases? The reason for this is that iron has an association with the magic mineral in that a residue of it does exist in iron ore as will be shown in chapter seven. They were not giving the children *exactly* what they needed but only a poor carrier of it. And carriers of the magic mineral can be imperfect because some carriers may have much less of the magic mineral than others. This is why the treatment was not completely successful. In the health/medical field the search is still on for the pica cure.

HOW DID SMOKING START?

So, as we've seen, there is a tradition that says pica is due to a nutritional 'gap', or deficiency, in one's diet. If this nutritional gap is filled with the right nutrient then pica behavior, including cigarette smoking, will stop. This is the underlying principle of this book. The right foods and/or supplements, which contain the missing nutrient, can halt all desire for the nonfood source, including tobacco and all the others mentioned in this chapter. Food can heal, or stop this reorientation of the human physiology.

But there is a profound paradox here. Food can solve the problem but food can also be the cause of the problem in the first place. This is where the careful distinction must be made between a food that is whole and food that is altered in some way. I call the latter a partial-food and what we see occurring at the beginning of the 20th century is the creation of a denatured food supply— partial-foods were born.

The 'man on the scene' that reported on this trend more than anyone else for that time period was a gentleman by the name of Alfred W. McCann. His view on the matter of food refining can be seen from the title of one of his books, *Starving America*, published in the year 1912. By that title he is not alluding to food shortages or the lack of food in this country. His thesis in this book was that Americans at that time had plenty of food to eat but that the food they were eating had been altered by an industrial process that was becoming widespread at the time. This altered food was causing massive starvation across America and he was sounding the alarm. He called this food alteration "crimes against our wheat, corn, rice and barley, against our biscuits, crackers and bread . . ."(pg. 26)

How was this food being altered and how could it cause starvation? According to McCann, the food that Americans were eating was "food from which a considerable proportion of nature's building materials have been extracted."(pg. 32) The 'building materials' that McCann is referring to are minerals which are part of the "fertile earth" which then become integrated into the "body of man" through the eating of certain foods like a "handful of wheat" which should contain the same minerals. He calls this process the "law of life". (pg. 28)

But the fact is, "these mineral salts are removed from our diet by commercial practices . . . and those who remove them have succeeded in establishing scientific justification for their work . . ." (pg. 47) This removal of valuable nutrients strikes at the heart of the problem of the American diet. Essential, staple foods are attacked in this process of refining. For example, cereal grains and their end-products (bread, pasta, biscuits etc.) are "units of denatured nutrition" due to this process of refining. The end-products even suffer a color change that signifies this denaturing of the original product and, as McCann intimates, this is not natural. "Nature never made a white grain of wheat . . ."

In chapter seven of *Starving America* he asks, "How does the white bread get white?" Now, his answer strikes at the core of this book, at the core of pica and, hence, at the core of cigarette smoking— and he happens to mention the magic mineral in his answer: "White bread gets white because from the ground grain of wheat three-fourths of the minerals, including the phosphorus, iron, lime, silica, sulfur, potassium and magnesium are removed. These elements are contained in the brown outer skin of the wheat berry, called the bran, and in the 'shorts', 'middlings' and 'tailings', which are sifted and bolted out of the ground meal, leaving principally the white starchy part of the interior part of the berry . . . the minerals which nature put into our wheat and which we so deliberately remove are lost to us forever and the vitalizing missions which they would have naturally and beneficently performed are never performed at all." (pg. 58, 60) The book you hold in your hand right now demonstrates that the "removal" of one of those nutrients causes reorientation in the individual to a nonfood source for that nutrient.

This removal of nutrients, in particular the magic mineral, is what mankind was—and still is—doing on a colossal scale. Hopefully, once you get through with this book (and apply it), you'll understand that the story of the removal of the Magic

Mineral in our society is as stupid and silly a thing to do as the world of the peel-eaters who removed the citrus fruit with its vitamins while retaining the nutrient-bereft peel. The parable of the peel-eaters is exactly the story of the twentieth century concerning the magic mineral. For reasons that will be revealed in chapter five, the human body can tolerate the loss of the other minerals for a short time but it can't tolerate the loss of the magic mineral at all. The human body will turn on a 'switch' and reorient itself to try to acquire this extremely important mineral through nonfoods, only some of which have been surveyed in this chapter.

All these strange habits and inclinations talked about in this chapter are all because of a missing nutrient due to pervasive food refining. If the magic mineral is removed on a large scale basis there will be reorientation, or pica, on a large scale basis.

This is precisely what we see in the first half of the 20th century. As a result of this widespread removal of the amazing mineral from the American diet, a "habit" developed in American culture that was so prevalent and deep-seated that it wasn't until the mid 1950s that it was even questioned— cigarette smoking. From the first decade of the twentieth century to the mid 1960s (the pinnacle of the white bread and white sugar era) there are some estimates that over 60 percent of Americans were smoking in that time period. Even if one only has a bare knowledge of popular culture for that sixty year period, the question could be asked— who wasn't smoking? Professional football coaches were smoking on the sidelines during games. Doctors were smoking in hospitals and so were patients! In fact, this was the era of the infamous ads in print and radio that touted: "According to a nationwide survey: More doctors smoke Camels than any other cigarette." But even in 'fake' life, like television and movies, everyone seemed to be grabbing a smoke. In real life hardly any place was smoke free— restaurants, airplanes, elevators, grocery stores, professional sports stadiums, offices, workplaces, hospitals, and even schools had smoking areas. Let's not forget the average home where children were subjected to second hand smoke all day. It seemed the whole world was puffing away!

The body was trying to mend the fracture in the food supply by reorienting to a nonfood which contained the magic mineral in a highly absorbable form, namely, tobacco smoke.

So, hand in hand with this explosion of food refining there was also the phenomenon of pica that was growing amongst the poor (clay and dirt eating) and middle and upper class (cigarette smoking). The partial-foods of refined grains and sugar, since they are stripped of the magic mineral, reoriented our physiology towards a nonfood that did contain the magic mineral in concentrated amounts.

But then something happened in the mid 1960s that changed this reorientation to tobacco. As a result of this circumstance, hordes of smokers began to try to quit smoking and many did. In fact, the percentage of smokers began to steadily decrease but another problem began to rear its head. Cigarette smokers, as a result of this event, began choosing an alternative source for the magic mineral— all the while thinking that they successfully quit smoking, the population chose a far worse pica object that we are still seeing the dreadful effects of.

CATCH 22

Certainly there were rumblings going on before this about the evil of smoking but it was in 1964 when the Surgeon Generals report came out that officially implicated cigarette smoking in cancer and other pathologies. Smokers listened and took this to heart and began trying to quit. But you can never 'quit' the magic mineral. You always need a source of this nutrient whether from whole food or nonfood sources because of its necessity in brain function (chapter 5).

As a result of this declaration from on high, the numbers began to reflect a steady decline in smoking— but something else was 'inclining'. There was an ascendancy of another pica object that the population of the world was choosing but this pica source was, and is, an extremely poor source of the magic mineral (in terms of health implications and amounts of the magic mineral). The "ex-smoker" was merely replacing one source (tobacco) of the magical mineral with another source that was, and still is, a less efficient carrier of the magic mineral and even worse for him or her healthwise.

This 'substitution' is exactly what began happening in the 1960's and it spawned a worldwide phenomenon known as obesity and all the problems associated with it. Why? Since this source does contain the magic mineral in very small amounts, consequently, *much more of this pica source must be consumed.*

This poorer source is nothing else but refined sugar and carbohydrates (chapter 7). As will be shown, refined sugar is a nonfood.

Another book could be written on the coincidence and parallels between the campaign against smoking and the co-incident rise in obesity but for our purposes we will use the timeline from 1964 to 2013. What we see from 1964 on is an outright war continually escalated against tobacco by the health/medical establishment until this very day when we see smoking bans in countries all around the world. Since that date smoking rates began to steadily drop— but something else increased. From 1964 to the year 2013, obesity has been the biggest problem at every age range and for every country. It was because the source that the population chose for the magic mineral had changed from tobacco.

Smokers who heeded the health warning, at that time, thought they were quitting but what inevitably happened was a redirection toward refined sugar as a source for the magic mineral— and this pica source is the main cause of obesity. The CDC has a breakdown of obesity rates for 12 to 19 year olds from the years 1963-65 compared to the years 2007-2008 and it is fascinating. That age range is one of the biggest smoking groups— that's when everyone starts, especially if we consider that, back in the 50's and 60's, smoking was considered 'cool'. Anyway, the CDC has the obesity rate for that age range at 4.6 percent in the years 1963-1965 and by 2007-2008 it had grown to 18.1 percent (CDC website article entitled *Prevalence of Obesity Among Children and Adolescents: United States, Trends 1963-1965 Through 2007-2008*). In the same time period the smoking rates have gone down across the board where they hover around 20 percent of the population in 2013 whereas in 1965, when the CDC began keeping records of smoking statistics, we see that 42.4 percent of the adult population were smoking.

YOU CAN'T QUIT THE MAGIC MINERAL

When social pressure and societal taboos are imposed upon individuals regarding a nonfood source most of these individuals will try to quit that source. And they might be successful even. As stated earlier you can't turn off the switch for the magic mineral. The individual will reorient and choose the pica object most handy to them and "socially acceptable".

And so this happened on a large scale in the second half of the twentieth century. Tobacco was declared an evil substance by the authority source and, to a great extent, people obeyed. But their bodies reoriented toward another pica source . . . *refined grains and refined sugars.*

Cereal grains and the sugar cane plant–when they are untouched by refining techniques–ironically are two of the richest sources of the magic mineral. But this richness of content is precisely why they can become a pica object. The magic mineral is not, and cannot be, completely removed in the refining process— a bare residue, a trace, remains. Also, strangely enough, what you will discover in chapter seven, is that the magic mineral is even *added back into refined sugar*, by processing methods, for the purpose of preserving and anti-caking. This does not make it 'whole' again but it can make it a pica source.

As a consequence of this minimal trace of the magic mineral left in the refined product, *more* of the product must be consumed. So when smokers began to 'quit', beginning in the late 1960s they turned to another source of the magic mineral. Once again, when social pressure prevents you from using a rich source of the magic mineral, your mind takes note but your body is on auto-pilot for the mineral and your body will switch to another source which is more socially acceptable. This is the great irony or duality— *even if you make the conscious choice to avoid one source, your body, on some other level, WILL make a choice for the Magic Mineral in another source.*

But this source has worse implications long term than even tobacco. Dr. David Reuben, author of *Everything You Always Wanted to Know About Nutrition* says about this pica source:

"...white refined sugar is not a food. It is a pure chemical extracted from plant sources, purer in fact than cocaine, which it resembles in many ways."(pg. 167) As we see Rueben's point demonstrated below, keep in mind that, to this day, the establishment has not attacked this nonfood with the zeal and ferocity that has been given to tobacco.

THE FIRE

In the middle of the 20th century Dr. William Coda Martin wrote that partial-foods cause an underlying condition known today as inflammation or the FIRE. When the individual consumes partial-foods, the body cannot 'interpret' this denatured food because it is missing vital components for incorporation into structures of the body. William Duffy, the author of the amazing book *Sugar Blues*, cites the journal known as *Michigan Organic News* (1957, March issue pg.3) in which Dr. Martin writes, "The body cannot utilize this refined starch and carbohydrate unless the depleted proteins, vitamins and minerals are present. Nature supplies these elements in each plant in quantities sufficient to metabolize the carbohydrate in that particular plant. There is no excess for other added carbohydrates. Incomplete carbohydrate metabolism results in the formation of 'toxic metabolite'."

Why does he call this end-product toxic? It is because the body sees it as an invader and, like a harmful pathogen entering the body, an immune response will take place . . . eventually. Generally, an immune system response to a foreign object–something that should not be in the body, be it a bacteria, virus, fungus, damaged cells, or some type of irritant– involves highly complex and intricate processes but in a broad sense it's very simple to understand. The invasive irritant causes the area to become lower in pH or more acidic. The body will respond by martialing its resources to bring more water (blood) to the FIRE (the acidic area) through these complex processes. *As a result of this process there will be an increase in size of the area affected.* This area then becomes known as inflamed— or *in-flames*, really.

Now, what you may have in mind after that simplified explanation is a local area such as, for example, your toe or a finger being swollen due to an infection from a cut or something. This is commonly understood to be an acute response which is short term but there is another type of inflammation, known as chronic type, that research has been showing is associated with disease in general and the "swelling" known as *obesity*. In the text *Inflammation, Lifestyle, and Chronic Disease* the scientists write that "excessive inflammation . . . is emerging as a fundamental initiator of most chronic human diseases, including cancer, diabetes, obesity, Alzheimer's disease, arthritis, and cardiovascular diseases."(from the preface)

Obesity is caused by inflammation and inflammation is caused by partial-foods. The cell can not fully metabolize this foreign agent, known as a partial-food, and because of this incomplete metabolism, the FIRE will eventually begin.

Dr. Robert H. Lustig, Professor of Clinical Pediatrics in the Division of Endocrinology and the Director of the Weight Assessment for Teen and Child Health (WATCH) Program at the University of California condemns the partial-food known as refined sugar. In a 2009 lecture entitled, *Sugar: The Bitter Truth*, Lustig calls refined sugar 'toxic' or 'poison' at least a dozen times. The New York Times magazine published an article on April 13, 2011 in which the author writes, "If Lustig is right, then our excessive consumption of sugar is the primary reason that the numbers of obese and diabetic Americans have skyrocketed in the past 30 years. But his argument implies more than that. If Lustig is right, it would mean that sugar is also the likely dietary cause of several other chronic ailments widely considered to be diseases of Western lifestyles — heart disease, hypertension and many common cancers among them."

The cell can't metabolize this foreign agent, known as partial-foods, and because of this incomplete metabolism, the FIRE will eventually begin and the eventual outcome will be obesity and/or related diseases. *What we must realize is that the food we eat, if it is devitalized or stripped of natural nutrients, can act as a foreign object to the body or, as Dr. Martin put it, toxic.* And anything that is toxic is sure to trigger the immune response known as inflammation.

As I said earlier, regular consumption of partial-foods spurs on inflammation . . . eventually. But before inflammation takes hold, the human body, in its intelligence, does something quite fascinating to avert it.

The rest of the world is engaging in far worse pica behavior than the smoker is. Tobacco actually alleviates inflammation while sugar does not. The smoker's choice of tobacco as pica object is more logical than any other pica object. The world has just turned up-side down.

CANNIBALISM

The human body acts with an intelligence that is astounding. At every point of the way there seems to be a protective software program that initiates a "plan" or procedure to meet with an existing condition in the cellular environment. One of the goals of this book is to demonstrate that cigarette smoking is one of those "plans" or procedures to allay inflammation—an intelligent response from the cellular environment. However, before the cell turns on the switch of reorientation to a pica source, it will undertake something that we view with disgust in the outside world but which occurs with regularity in the "inside world" of the cellular environment— cannibalism.

The most important characteristic of a whole food is that it carries within it the elements necessary for incorporation into the body. For food to become "you" it must have these components to carry out incremental biochemical changes which result in the food being assimilated into your very structure. This biochemical process, where food becomes "you", is known as metabolization. But partial-food is just that— partial. It does not have the necessary 'keys' to pass through the gates of metabolization. It is missing those elements due to the refining process. This will eventually result in the FIRE, the inflammation response. But before the body uses this tool of inflammation to fix this problem, an amazing thing happens.

To fix a picture of this "amazing thing" in our heads, to simplify it, we must picture the cell as being a gatekeeper that asks each molecule of food, "Do you have the necessary keys to pass through?" A whole food says "yes" to this but a partial-food does not have the keys to pass— they are fragmented and incomplete. Here is what is amazing— the gatekeeper (the cell), being flexible and not wanting to cause trouble (inflammation), says to the partial-food, "Well, since you're here and since I don't want you breaking the door down to get in (inflammation) I'll see what I can do" The gatekeeper then borrows the necessary pieces from friends of his that will make the keys of the partial-food molecules complete so it can become whole and so that it can pass and be assimilated into the structure of the body.

But where does the body, or the cell, borrow from? From itself. In essence, because a partial-food is incapable of being metabolized fully, it becomes the cause of further or *secondary nutrient depletion*. This means that the cell borrows from certain structures in the body that are lower in the hierarchical system in order to prevent a worse situation from breaking out.

However, this borrowing is only meant to be temporary. It is a backup plan but it requires attacking and utilizing the stores of the body for use in metabolization. In other words, when you eat a refined carbohydrate, like sugar or refined grain, your body must borrow vital nutrients from healthy cells and structures to metabolize the incomplete food you are taking in. Calcium, sodium, potassium and magnesium, and various other nutrients, are taken from various parts of the body to metabolize or make use of the fractioned food. It is a sort of *micro-cannibalization*. In contrast, any food that is whole, that has not been refined, does not impose this reorganization upon the body because the whole food contains these nutrients already in its structure.

We can see where this could lead. The body has a limited supply of these co-factors of metabolism such as minerals. The consumption of partial-foods forces you to 'dip into a limited bank account.' When you overdraw on this account then pathologies of various kinds will set in. Minerals, for instance, not only are structural components of body organs and tissues, they are necessary in physiological processes such as osmotic pressure, acid-base balance and transmission of nerve impulses—not to mention their function in catalytic systems as enzyme components or activators of enzyme systems. Blah-blah-blah. Here's the important point you need to know: If these minerals are missing then we will see a correspondence of decline in these systems and structures of the body. Eating partial-foods requires the body to cannibalize itself, to steal from these vital systems and structures.

If you don't want to read the evidence for this just skip to the next section. In short, the evidence reveals that the body steals elements from somewhere in the body in order to process the partial-food.

There are many examples of this 'cannibalization' in the scientific literature. If you don't want to read the evidence for this just skip to the next section. In short, the evidence reveals that the body steals elements from somewhere in the body in order to process the partial-food.

Anyway, let's start with the journal *Metabolism* (Volume 35, Issue 6, June 1986, pages 515-518) in which a study was conducted with 37 people involving two diets. For 12 weeks they were on a reference diet "formulated by nutritionists to contain optimal levels of protein, carbohydrates and fat and other nutrients." The following 6 weeks they were on a less than optimal diet that was high in sugar. This particular study was fashioned to examine and study one nutrient— the mineral known as chromium. The contents of both diets had the same amount of chromium. After all was said and done the conclusions of the study were somewhat astounding. The high sugar diet saw chromium urinary excretion rates of 300% while on the first diet which had less sugar the excretion rates of chromium were 10%. The authors of the study conclude: "These data demonstrate that consumption of diets high in simple sugars stimulates chromium losses . . ."

But where on earth is that extra chromium coming from in

that high sugar diet? The startling conclusion is that it may be coming from stores in the body. In other words, in order for that sugar to be processed by the cell and become incorporated into the structure of the human body it needs other factors, one of which is chromium. Since that sugar does not contain chromium it must borrow it from already existing structures in your body. Soon you will become depleted of this important mineral and many others.

In the *Journal of Nutrition* (Volume 113: 1335-1345, 1983) a study was done in which rats were fed a sucrose diet that was already deficient in copper. The strange thing that was discovered was that the high sucrose diet further decreased the levels of copper in the mice. "Feeding sucrose . . . magnified the copper deficiency and resulted in 60% mortality . . . the hepatic copper concentration of rats fed sucrose was reduced nearly threefold . . ." So, here is an example of another mineral, copper, which gets depleted from your body when you ingest partial-foods. Minerals are being lost and eventually excreted after consuming partial-foods.

In the *European Journal of Nutrition* (October 2007) a study entitled, *Implications of oxidative stress in high sucrose low magnesium fed rats,* was published in which it was found that "Levels of various antioxidants fell significantly in plasma of HS (high sucrose) rats." The reason for the fall is that they are being used up to metabolize the partial-food. A partial-food must steal nutrients from the body in order to become 'whole' again, so to speak.

Obviously, this situation can not last forever, for the body is limited in these reserves and when this happens the partial-foods will not be able to be incorporated. At this point the 'toxic metabolite' that Dr. Martin referred to, the FIRE, is formed. According to Dr. Martin this by-product of incomplete metabolization " . . . accumulates in the brain and nervous system . . . these toxic metabolites interfere with the respiration of the cells. They cannot get sufficient oxygen to survive and function normally. In time some of the cells die. This interferes with the function of a part of the body and is the beginning of degenerative disease."

Ultimately, it's a downward spiral with partial-foods. First, the body cannibalizes itself in order to provide co-factors to metabolize the partial-food. This strategy is to prevent, as long as possible, the inflammatory response. This strategy of the body probably coincides with a certain time period, possibly the pre-teen years. Second, when further cannibalization is no longer possible the inflammatory process, the FIRE, begins at the cellular level. Third, because of the FIRE, the cell reorients itself to obtain the natural FIRE- extinguisher in a nonfood form . . . the magic mineral through pica.

This last strategy also probably coincides with a time period, namely the teen and early adulthood years, which is when the smoking habit normally begins in order to mitigate against the inflammation. One phase leads to another.

WHAT'S THE POINT?

Pica is an emergency response. When a person turns to a nonfood for the magic mineral it is not meant to be a permanent remedy. All pica objects will have long-term negative consequences. However, if we were to have a rating system for the different pica sources and compare the same, the conclusion would have to be reached that *refined grains and sugars are far worse than tobacco smoking.* These so-called foods systematically plunder the body of much needed nutrients and then, after they are done robbing and stealing, they create an inflammatory state which is the basis for most disease and obesity. The point of this whole demostration is to say that the enemy is not tobacco. The twentieth century was the century of partial-foods which caused the pica response: in the first half of the century it was tobacco as the pica object and in the second half of the 20th century and into the 21st, the population has made the choice for a far poorer source of the magic mineral. Keep in mind that this latter result is all due to an authority decrying one pica source (tobacco) which the population, on a conscious level, obeyed. On a deeper, cellular plane the body can't 'quit' the amazing mineral and reorientation toward another source WILL occur.

The point is that the world is pointing the finger at smokers while overlooking a far greater problem. Many nonsmokers have a log stuck in their eye while complaining about the little splinter of the smokers, as the saying goes. The ultimate cause of pica–partial-foods–is given a free pass by the establishment, except for some like Dr. Lustig. The next time you hear someone making a crack about smokers or see someone giving that 'high and mighty' look toward someone who is smoking, check to see if he is stuffing his face with a donut.

SMOKING IS LOGICAL

The pica list is surely strange: chalk, laundry detergent, talcum powder, raw rice, clay, refined sugar, tobacco, etc,. But ALL of these items have ONE element in them that the human body, especially the brain, is seeking. The magic mineral has very special properties when it comes to balancing the internal environment of the body and of the individual cell. The foremost of these characteristics is its anti-inflammatory abilities— it is the great FIRE extinguisher. This is why it is sought out in any form, even if that form may cause collateral damage long term. In inflammatory, acidic surroundings, the individual cells face an unconventional circumstance and this invokes the response of pica which, on the surface, looks rather unconventional.

By now there may be a concerned furrow on your brow. How can smoking tobacco be an anti-inflammatory? There's a rather strange thing that has been found by scientists concerning the brains of smokers. A study that was published in the Proceedings of the National Academy of Sciences (PNAS) reported on this "strange thing" in a paper dauntingly entitled, *Brain monoamine oxidase A inhibition in cigarette smokers* (PNAS 1996 November 26; 93(24): 14065–14069). Smokers, according to the study, are lacking certain enzymes that break down certain neurotransmitters. "Smokers had significantly lower brain MAO A than nonsmokers in all brain regions examined."

Surely, 'lower' can't mean 'good', right? In this case, 'lower' does mean good. If you compare a smoker with a nonsmoker the nonsmoker will usually have *more* of an enzyme called monoamine oxidase A in their brain and the smoker will have less of that enzyme. But this is a good thing *for the smoker* because having more of this enzyme, which the nonsmoker does, is linked with depression. The researchers concluded that there is something in tobacco smoke that "clears out" this enzyme so that it is barely around in the smokers brain. The authors of the study write that "it is possible that tobacco smoke may have antidepressant properties." Notice they say "tobacco smoke" and not an element of tobacco smoke such as nicotine. There is *something else* in that tobacco smoke that is suppressing this enzyme which causes depression and it is not nicotine according to these researchers: "It has also been demonstrated that nicotine is not responsible for MAO A inhibition."

Now that we have that little intro out of the way, we'll look at why this enzyme is linked to depression. It turns out that when this enzyme is activated to "do its job" of breaking down neurotransmitters, there is something released into the extra-cellular environment as a result of this breakdown process. According to another study published in PNAS entitled *Monoamine oxidase A and repressor R1 are involved in apoptotic signaling pathway* (vol. 103 no. 29 Xiao-Ming Ou, 10923–10928), the thing released from this enzyme that is just "doing its job", ultimately results in cell death: "Monoamine oxidase A (MAO A) degrades serotonin, norepinephrine, and dopamine and produces reactive oxygen that may cause neuronal cell death." Reactive oxygen is not a good thing because it is an inflammatory affect as the following study confirms: "Inflammatory reactions induce the production of reactive oxygen species (ROS): the reverse sequence of these events is also true." (*Reactive oxygen species and inflammation* C R Seances Soc Biol Fil. 1993;187(3):286-95)

Reactive oxygen is a by-product of inflammation. Monoamine oxidase A causes reactive oxygen to occur. Monoamine oxidase A is missing in smokers or, is not as abundant as in nonsmokers. These studies lead us to the conclusion that *something in tobacco smoke is preventing inflammation because smokers don't have as much of the catalyst for inflammation, MAO A, as nonsmokers do.*

Here's the deal: These enzymes that are more present in nonsmokers act like vacuum cleaners. Their job is to clean up 'dirt' (unused neurotransmitters) and dispose of it. Smoker's brains are 'clean' by contrast and don't need these junk disposers known as MAO A and MAO B. There's less 'junk' to clean up in the smoker's brain.

PARADOX EXPLAINED

But it does seem like a paradox of sorts— the body desperately needs the magic mineral and yet it chooses a source (any pica object) that could, down the road, do damage to it? This dichotomy should not seem so strange to us when we think about it a little. This action or reorientation toward a possibly destructive nonfood mirrors emergency situations that individuals have faced in real life. For example, if an individual is locked in a room in a house where there is a raging fire, he or she wouldn't hesitate too much about breaking a window with their bare hands, if there is no other object handy to break that window. The person will risk injury to the body in breaking the window with a punch. Would a person in ordinary day to day circumstances go around smashing his fist through any window he sees? We would think this behavior rather strange and 'unconventional' wouldn't we?

But we can envision a situation when this behavior would be 'right'. In a raging inferno the person in trouble needs oxygen and doesn't care, for the moment, about cuts and gashes from punching that window. This is a mirror of how the cell acts in an emergency such as inflammation. It doesn't care where it gets the magic mineral, just as long as it gets it— like the much needed oxygen for that person trapped in that room. The brain has a single-minded purpose for that 'oxygen', the magic mineral, and it will risk long-term injury to do so.

Look, breaking a window with your fist is really not 'doctor recommended'. Obviously, smoking isn't either.

But the doctor may not see or understand (or does not want to see) the context— that the fire is not so ideal either. The person smashes that window in with his fist because there is a desperate and perilous situation around him. There is a great deal of ignorance about the situation, the context, surrounding the issue of why a person smokes. This involves ignorance about the tobacco plant and ignorance about inflammation and its effects. As strange as it may sound, smoking–all pica in general–is a protective mechanism against inflammation and inflammation is due to partial-foods. It is a quite logical reaction to an emergency situation. To solve the problem requires knowing more about what caused the emergency situation.

SUMMARY

Here is the order of how things happen:

1) Consumption of food that has the magic mineral missing leads to

2) The body turning on the mechanism by which it obtains this mineral somewhere/ somehow else in the immediate environment

3) Humans find many different sources for this mineral in their environment. These include, but are not limited to, clay and dirt, laundry detergent, ice cubes, refined sugar, and tobacco.

They are all carriers of the magic mineral.

Everyone needs this mineral for brain function. No one can escape. The body, acting intelligently, is trying to mend a fracture in the food supply.

Our civilization views the problem of smoking, and the pica response in general, with an out of focus lense. Because the underlying cause, the final cause, is completely ignored. Partial-foods that are devoid of the magic mineral cause the inflammation which causes the pica response.

The great and sad irony is that the pica response (smoking, eating clay, etc) is blamed when really it is a response to mitigate or lessen the load of inflammation.

There is a much deeper and wider story here. There is much more to the iceberg than we can see. Being able to see the problem in a wider context will enable us to seek the real solutions. The smoking problem is very small in scale compared to the bigger issue; it is only a small subset of a far greater problem.

CHAPTER 3: PARADIGM LOST

Tobacco is not the villain. In fact, it serves its purpose well by offering to the smoker a highly absorbable source of a very important mineral that has been removed from our food supply. Thanks to refining techniques and, also, current dietary fads, this mineral is prevented from becoming a staple in the modern diet. Because of this scarcity, the cell suffers from *specific hunger* and, as a result, the human body turns on the "switch" of *reorientation* towards a nonfood, which for many people happens to be tobacco. By consuming a nonfood, the human body is trying to mend a fracture in the food supply.

In this light, smoking, or the pica response in general, is seen as an intelligent response to scarcity of a nutrient that happens to be fundamental in brain function. In short, chronic deficiency of the magic mineral leads to smoking or other various pica responses.

Nutrient deficiency as the cause of smoking?

It may come as a surprise but nutrient deficiency due to partial-food consumption was, at various times in medical history, the primary apparatus used in interpreting physical and, as we shall see, mental afflictions. And it proved to be an absolute success . . . whenever it was used.

The medical establishment in the first half of the 20th century was successful in curing at least two major physical diseases because it followed (by force of circumstance) the interpretive framework of nutrient deficiency due to partial-foods consumption. The theory of treating a nutrient deficiency "worked"—the diseases were cured because the origin, the ultimate cause, was discovered.

Compare this to the modern era. It seems we have digressed, instead of progressed, by abandoning this paradigm because in our time almost every treatment for a disease is *symptomatic treatment*.

Symptomatic treatment is the modern way. It simply means "doing away with the symptom" without treating the cause, the origin, of that symptom. Most of the time a picture can drive home the point better. The "cure" for body odor is soap and water. If we apply the modern symptomatic treatment to this problem then we would get a "prescription" for special perfume to be filled at the local pharmacy to solve the problem. But, I think you can see, sooner or later the root of the problem is going to rear its ugly head. The "perfume prescription" is only masking the real problem. In essence, modern medical treatments just tell you to put the perfume on instead of diagnosing and treating the cause.

In the smoking cessation field that is all there is— symptomatic treatment. The examples that parade about us in books, internet, and television are endless. Everything but the kitchen sink is thrown at us— hypnotism, nicotine replacement therapy, neuro-linguistic programming, willpower and self-confidence counseling and even drugs that are meant to take away the cravings. Every treatment modality has their own theory as to why you are smoking yet the cause as to why you smoke has not been found. Not to mention they are all in "percentage-land" (refer to chapter 1)

Partial-foods create the original problem, the fracture. The physical body, the mind, and even society is impacted by this fracture and the only solution to mending it is by recognizing what first caused it. Until we 'fix' the partial-food problem, which marginalizes this very important mineral, we should not 'blame' the strategy that the body uses to deal with the fracture. That strategy, the pica response of smoking, or any other pica response, is nearly insignificant and dwarfed by the much larger issue as we shall now see.

I just want you to see how much of a success the paradigm of nutrient deficiency can be by looking at a couple of times in history when it was used to cure actual physical disease. Today, because of the prevailing paradigm, these diseases would never have been cured.

Also, I want you to notice in the following that these physical diseases caused a *reaction known as pica*. Remember the order from chapter two. Nutrient deficiency causes . . . Inflammation . . . which causes disease . . . which causes Pica. And the pica happens to be for the magic mineral.

GERMS VS. NUTRIENT DEFICIENCY

In the second half of the 19th century there was urgency in the air because the ravages of the disease known as *kakke* was spreading to parts of Japanese society that were critical in Japan's future amongst the nations: the Japanese navy recruits were dying. Kanehiro Takaki, the Japanese doctor commissioned to look into this disease, reported that in 1870 about 75 percent of the patients in the Naval hospital were suffering from kakke. He also noted that this disease had similarities to another disease that was ravaging the lands across the waters in Southeast Asia.

At first, Western doctors were mystified by kakke because the vantage point that they were looking from in interpreting this disease was in terms of infection or germs. The germ theory was starting to take hold in the Western world and many of the scientists eagerly sought to explain kakke as some sort of infection.

This interpretive viewpoint was the case in the late 19th century in the Dutch colonies as well, where the same disease was breaking out amongst some of the inhabitants but mostly the Dutch military that were stationed there. A commission of doctors and pathologists were called in to try and halt the onslaught of *beriberi* as they called it.

First they inspected the nerve tissue of deceased patients and animals to try and isolate the disease— but they couldn't find any specific bacteria to isolate. Because of their belief in the germ theory they continued in their investigation by taking the blood of 'infected patients' and injecting it into monkeys, rabbits and dogs. The animals were expected to 'come down' with the disease . . . . but they didn't. So multiple injections were tried and finally the animals came down with some nerve degeneration but it was debated whether that was from the blood or from an infection due to multiple injections, as these animals developed abscesses at the point of injection.

Because the results were not conclusive, it led the leader of the commission to conclude that beriberi was a rather bizarre example of an infectious disease because it required multiple exposures for the host to become infected. The germ theory, which would soon come to prevail in the entire world, was not providing the answers in this case and Western, along with Japanese doctors, remained perplexed. A different paradigm was needed.

GOVERNMENT DISEASE

The story of beriberi and its eventual solution could really be called 'A Tale of Two Cooks'. Christian Eijkman, who was put in charge of investigating the disease after the commission disbanded, noticed that his chickens were developing symptoms that were similar to beriberi. These chickens were being used to test the germ theory of beriberi so they were regularly being injected with infected blood from those who died from beriberi. A strange thing happened however— some chickens fell ill *without being injected*. Eijkman believed the air of his lab was now infected with germs so he moved away from the lab and decided to start anew with a fresh batch of chickens. However, something even stranger happened— the chickens that had fallen ill at the previous lab that he thought was infected, had *recovered completely from the disease*. In exasperation he wrote, " all material for further experiments fell away."

Amazingly, Eijkman kept at it and it paid off, for something came to his attention which seemed promising for the solution of beriberi. He wrote: "Something struck us that had escaped our attention so far." This 'something' was the story of two cooks. It came to Eijkmans attention that the food of the chickens in his experiments had changed without him being aware of it. The man Eijkman had put in charge of the chickens for their daily fare and care had made a deal with the cook of the military hospital to provide leftover rice to him for the chickens. This cook was replaced five months later with another cook who did not agree with this arrangement. As Eijkman wrote, this new cook "had seen no reason to give military rice to civilian hens." So the chickens had to do with the rice that they had before the change. What struck Eijkman was that the time periods of the chickens becoming ill correlated with the change in the diet. When they were eating the rice from the hospital they became ill and showed signs of beriberi. This was the same rice being fed to the military and government employees and these were the people who were suffering to a greater extent than the natives—this led one writer to call the disease a 'government disease'. When the chickens went back to eating the non-hospital rice they actually became better.

In Southeast Asia and in Japan there were two forms of rice that were eaten by the people. There was white rice which had the husk or outer shell removed along with the next layer of skin which is called the pericarp or 'silverskin'. This was the rice that was being fed to the military and government personnel. It was also preferred by the wealthy in some areas such as Thailand. The other rice is known as brown rice which has the 'silverskin' still attached to the endosperm. This was the traditional way of eating the rice and it was the way the poor amongst the natives ate their rice.

What Eijkman found out was that the chickens recovered when they ate the brown rice which was their original feed until the man in charge of the chickens struck the deal with the cook at the military hospital, giving them white rice. As soon as they ate the white rice the chickens began developing signs of beriberi. To Eijkman, this meant that there must be some factor in the 'silverskin' that is vital to human and animal nutrition. It was confirmed in other cases as well as when prisoners in the military prisons of Java were coming down with beriberi.

What was the common factor? Those prisons that were serving white rice had far higher incidences of beriberi than the prisons which were serving brown rice with the silverskin intact. One group, the prisons with higher incidence of beriberi, was eating a partial-food— white rice, while the other group, those seemingly 'immune' to beriberi, was eating the whole food— brown rice.

Though it wasn't until a few years later, the factor was eventually isolated by scientists. Today we understand that the factor that was missing in the white rice is a vitamin— thiamine or vitamin B1. The physiological effects of this vitamin missing in the diet can be extremely serious. They range from nervous system damage to edema and congestive heart failure and eventually death.

We can now begin to see the devastation of a partial-food such as the processed rice that was being eaten in that part of the world in that time period. Because of this awareness, governments across the world began to fortify foods that were processed, with B vitamins such as thiamine. If they didn't add these you can be sure within a short period of time there would be another outbreak of beriberi. But with our contemporary germ/infection frame of mind how would we look at it? Probably as a virus or some type of infectious outbreak. Just keep in mind it was only one nutrient that caused this devastation which ranged from complaints of tiredness to actual death.

THE MAGIC MINERAL PUTS OUT THE FIRE

Beriberi was really a worldwide occurrence. In hindsight, medical historians realize that throughout the world beriberi was being described by doctors in various places who were just naming it differently. One such place and time period is the Caribbean during the 19th century. Kenneth Kiple in his book

The Caribbean Slave relates how the exact same symptoms were being described by physicians who treated slaves except they called it *mal d' estomach*. The treatment, according to Kiple, that was prescribed at the time was a "nutritious diet" that included fresh meat. The interesting thing is that meat is rich in B-1 or thiamine. What is more interesting, however, is what Kiple reports the physicians concluded about the disease. "The most common explanation viewed the disease as caused by pica usage or dirt eating."

The physicians noticed that a high percentage of those who were suffering the disease were engaging in pica and therefore believed the cause to be pica. We do the same thing today with tobacco when we impute the cause of diseases to cigarette smoking while actually it is only a reaction to an underlying condition. The pica occurring in these people, the desire for clay, was actually a reaction due to an inflammatory condition caused by a partial-food. A partial-food because it did not contain vitamin B-1 or thiamine. In order to adapt to this, the slaves engaged in pica to alleviate the symptoms. But there is no vitamin B-1 in clay. If this is so then why would the slaves be eating clay? It is because clay contains the magic mineral and it is the universal FIRE-extinguisher. *Any* nutrient deficiency will create inflammation and the magic mineral is the all-purpose FIRE-fighter as will be shown in chapter five.

In the book *The American Health Dilemma(* volume one), the authors make an interesting comment about beriberi in the slave population in the United States during the 18th century. On page 226 of their book they state that the slaves " . . . suffered from a spectrum of thiamine deficiency *leading to dirt/clay eating* or to full blown beriberi." (italics mine) Again, there is no thiamine in dirt or clay. The physicians, of that time period, reported on beriberi and how they associated this habit of clay eating occurring hand in hand with the deficiency or disease. So here we have another reference to pica occurring along with a disease state— and disease is inflammation (chapter 2). These slaves had no access to tobacco and since clay also contains the magic mineral they were using it to mitigate against the effects of their disease state.

What those slaves were actually doing was treating their condition, due to partial-foods consumption, by the pica response. What we must grasp is that one occurs because of the other. Pica (clay eating, cigarette smoking, etc) is caused by an internal inflammatory condition which in turn is due to a specific nutritional deficiency (consuming partial-foods). If there is no inflammation then there will be no pica.

Once again, the strangeness and uniqueness of the magic mineral is this: the disease beriberi is a B1 deficiency—but the body is not seeking B-1 in the environment through pica— it is seeking the magic mineral. Wouldn't it be better to reorient the body to acquire items that have B-1? This is an impossibility with most nutrients; *they are not as ubiquitous in nature as the magic element is.* As if by design, the magic mineral is omnipresent in our environment. Because of this availability, it suits the emergency condition of inflammation. Other nutrients do not have this universality and, hence, availability about them.

PRESCRIPTION FILLED YET AGAIN

Another disease, pellagra, was known as a form of leprosy, so devastating was its effect on the human form. This disease, at different periods of time, ravaged Europe and was especially virulent in the American South up until the 1920's. A New

York Times article from 1909, echoing the opinion of doctors at the time, called it "one of the most horrible pitiful afflictions mankind has ever suffered from." This was not just a skin disease however– it was a killer. In the first ten months of the year 1915 there were 1,306 deaths due to pellagra in South Carolina alone. So this was a disease that not only manifested as a severe skin affliction but also what was described as "the four D's": diarrhea, dermatitis, dementia and . . . . death. In the South, in 1916, there were over 100,000 affected. Because of the entrenchment of the disease for quite some time in the South, a hospital was founded in 1914 dedicated specifically to curing pellagra.

What is interesting about this disease is that the researchers and especially the primary researcher, Joseph Goldberger, had a completely different outlook on this disease, at the outset, than the researchers of beriberi. With beriberi we saw that the germ theory took hold at the beginning of investigations. But the theory was unfruitful in finding a cure.

With pellagra, Goldberger was looking, from the very beginning, for a nutritional deficiency. But this presupposition of his was heavily influenced by the work of those who eventually discovered that beriberi was a nutritional deficiency. Even though there was widespread belief that it might be some type of germ or a poison in a food item, such as the Times article just cited speculated, Goldberger stuck to his assumption of a nutritional deficiency.

Using volunteers from a prison, Goldberger was able to induce pellagra in the prisoners within two to three weeks by feeding them a poor diet. Partial-foods once again as the cause. He cured the pellagra by giving the prisoners whole foods— fresh fruits and vegetables. Eventually the cause was found to be a deficiency in the vitamin known as Niacin or vitamin B-3.

Here again, with pellagra, we notice a strange concurrence. When it was epidemic, physicians noted that another thing seemed to go hand in hand with the disease— clay eating. In volume 90 of the *Journal of the Royal Society of Medicine* (Nov. 1997) the authors of an article on pellagra cite research in which they conclude that there has been something 'overlooked': "An often overlooked aspect of pellagra is that *pica may occur concurrently*." (emphasis mine)

Pica is a response to the inflammatory condition of the disease state. The cell needs the FIRE-fighter, the magic mineral, to help mitigate the situation. In other words, all forms of pica (including cigarette smoking) are a *reaction* to inflammation occurring at the cellular level. Inflammation has grades of seriousness from low to high levels. At the high end of the spectrum we would see a disease manifestation. But every level is caused by partial-foods consumption or just a simple need for the magic mineral. And every level of the inflammation spectrum needs the magic mineral to deal with the FIRE. Therefore, at every level we will see pica in one of its forms.

PELLAGRA OF THE BRAIN

Abram Hoffer began his career as a clinical psychiatrist in Canada. What he proposed was that psychiatric disease and mental problems in general were due to a nutritional deficiency, or as he called it 'dependency', on the right molecules such as vitamins, minerals and amino acids. This was and still is a radical position but the problem, at least for the establishment at that time, was that Hoffer had the evidence to back it up.

We just discussed the ravages of pellagra and how it is cured by taking niacin or vitamin B-3. What Hoffer noticed is that the last stage of pellagra, before a person finally succumbed to it, was mental illness. Remember, pellagra is known as the disease with the four D's: diarrhea, dermatitis, dementia and death. The dementia that was in pellagra patients before they died resembled the symptoms that Hoffer was seeing in his psychiatric practice with schizophrenia patients. He theorized that schizophrenia was *actually a form of pellagra*, a transition state, without the other physical symptoms such as dermatitis. So he administered the vitamin B-3 to his patients and a strange thing happened— they recovered from a *mental* disease that previously had a grim prognosis.

In February of 1952, Hoffer treated his first case, a 17 year old boy admitted to Saskatchewan Hospital. He was diagnosed as being an acute case of schizophrenia. As Hoffer states in his book *Healing Schizophrenia*, "he was excited , silly, and at times deluded. He responded only occasionally to ECT (electro-shock) . . . During the next three weeks, his condition deteriorated to the point where he required complete nursing care." This was the route that Hoffer saw so many go down until he decided to try a new approach: "In May, he was started on 5 grams of niacin (B-3) and 5 grams of ascorbic acid (vitamin C) divided into 5 daily doses. Within 24 hours he was better, and 10 days later he was described as almost normal. We stopped giving him vitamins a month later and observed him in hospital for three weeks before he was discharged to his home in July. A follow-up three years later showed that he was in good health and had finished his final year of school." Keep in mind that B-3 or niacin was the cure found for pellagra.

Hoffer conducted six clinical trials between 1952 and 1960 with each one being a success. The group treated with vitamins always improved while the groups receiving placebo did not. The results were so uniform and so dramatic that Hoffer and his associates could barely contain their enthusiasm for this 'new' treatment. They feared that their exhilaration was "being conveyed to our patients and coloring the results" so they instead used "uninterested and skeptical doctors" to administer the vitamin protocol to the patients. If something is true it doesn't matter whose hand it is in, as Hoffer found out: "The results nearly five years later were similar to ours."

Hoffer was restoring to the patients vital nutrients that were not available in the partial-foods they were eating. These elements of nutrition were and are processed out of the foods— especially in Hoffer's day, from the 1940's to the early 1970's, when refined sugar was practically touted as a health food in all the media outlets including national magazines such as LIFE and TIME.

For example, there's a full page ad in TIME from March 4, 1966, in which you can see an effervescent young girl swinging about excitedly alongside some text written next to her about how much she accomplished in a particular day only through the consumption of refined sugar. As the ad says, "She needs sugar in her life. For energy . . . . Sugar swings. Serve some." And then a 'Note to mothers' at the bottom of the ad: "Exhaustion may be dangerous . . . Exhaustion opens the door a little wider to the bugs and ailments that are always lying in wait. Sugar puts back energy fast— offsets exhaustion. Energy is the first requirement of life. Play safe with your young ones— make sure they get sugar every day." This is just a taste of how much these partial-foods were especially embedded in our diet in this time period which also happened to coincide with the greatest usage of tobacco.

A PLAGUE THAT EATS

Language can, in a funny way, sometimes reveal truths that lay submerged in a culture. How many times have we heard or said things like "What's eating you? and "It's eating away at me!" The fascinating thing is that these statements represent a valid physiological condition. We now know that the human body takes a catabolic downturn when it is emotionally and mentally stressed. Psychological stress induces the release of the hormone cortisol which, among other things, will ultimately break down protein from muscle sources in your body to use as energy.

The body is literally eating itself when stressed.

The greatest mental health issue in the 20th century (and counting) was the problem of *stress*. *The reason for this was due to the removal of the magic mineral from the food supply.* The whole issue of stress should be turned on its head. We are not more stressed out than previous generations or civilizations. Rather, we are more deficient in the magic mineral which is the greatest anti-stress nutrient because it is a nutrient of the mind. Because of this, the organism turns to nonfood items that contain the magic mineral. This also is the story of the 20th century and beyond. The general population turned to smoking (for the magic mineral) which *reduced stress.*

Stress is called the Modern Plague but it uncannily corresponds to the 'Modern Food Processing Techniques' that have abounded for over 100 years. In other words, what if we have it all backwards? What if it's the other way around? It just may be that we have this thing called stress *because* of the partial-foods that have been introduced into society since the beginning of the 20th century.

THE UNIVERSAL FIRE EXTINGUISHER

If mental illness is what Abram Hoffer and others have demonstrated it to be, an inflammatory condition due to partial-foods consumption, then we will see pica occurring through the whole spectrum of mental illness.

When examining the whole range of mental illness, whether it is stress, depression or full blown schizophrenia, there seems to be an ineluctable association with pica that is relative to the degree of mental illness. In other words, the more serious the mental illness, the greater the intensity of the pica. The brain is simply trying to alleviate a possibly worsening situation by searching for the magic mineral which is in all pica substances. In the June 1993 edition of the *British Journal of Psychiatry*, the authors report in an article on depression and pica, "The case of a person . . . whose pica became uncontrollable during episodes of depressive illness." A correlation can be seen here between a state of the brain (depression) and a degree of pica.

In 1992 the psychiatrists Brenda and William Parry-Jones published a survey of pica from the historical aspect in the *British Journal of Psychiatry*. After reviewing the literature concerning the correspondence between severe mental illness and pica the authors state that, "Pica in the mentally disordered and the mentally retarded was referred to regularly in the 19th century asylum case notes and in textbooks on insanity." This is an accepted fact in the psychiatric profession, even today, as the authors from the French psychiatric journal *Le' Encephale* say in the Sept-Oct 2003 edition: "Indeed, pica is often a secondary diagnosis associated with other psychiatric conditions characterized by profound mental deterioration."

Pica is acute in schizophrenics. It has been known for some time that the incidence of smoking in schizophrenics is far greater than that in the general population. In the December, 1992 edition of the journal *Schizophrenia Research* the authors of the article *Smoking and Schizophrenia* state: "Several studies have shown that patients with schizophrenia have an extremely high prevalence of smoking, almost 90%, compared to only 33% in the general population . . ."

What many authorities understand by pica is the eating of a nonfood item. This is not correct. As stated in chapter two, there is precedent for the expansion of this term. In fact, Parry-Jones cites the German physician J.H. Cohausen from the 17th century, as classifying 'snuff', which is a tobacco powder taken through the nose, as a form of pica. This is only to say that when the medical journals say 'pica' they mean only substances that are ingested into the body through the mouth. Historically, the correct definition of pica should be the willful entry of any substance, in any form, into any entry point of the body that allows for incorporation and metabolism.

CRIMINAL BEHAVIOR AND PARTIAL-FOODS

The Qolla people of Incawatana posed a problem for the anthropologist, Ralph Bolton. The typical sociological theories were bandied about by previous investigators but each one fell short in explanation. The tribal elders of the group could not understand it either. As one of them told Bolton, "No es racional, pues!"— that is, 'A rational person could not do things like that'.

There were a good many anthropologists that came before Bolton that studied this group and they all came to a general conclusion. Pertti Pelto, one of those anthropologists, summarized the research into this group of people: "In the anthropological literature, these Andean highlanders are portrayed as perhaps the meanest and most unlikable people on the earth."

What's more, they were characterized as such ever since their encounter with Western civilization. As far back as the 16th century, we have Padre Martin de Murua, a Mercedarian friar, describing the Qolla as "brutos y torpos." In other words, 'irrational', 'cruel', and 'uncivilized' or 'stupid'.

Bolton was astounded at the present situation in 1970. After gathering the evidence he came to the startling conclusion that the Qolla, statistically, were *the most violent people on earth.* He calculated the homicide rate across a time period of 25 years (from 1945 to 1969) at 55 per 100,000 people whereas all other societies in the world ranged from rates of .3 to 34 per 100,000 people. In a fifteen year period, the village authorities kept careful records of disputes and various crimes. Through examining the cases during this period, Bolton realized that the highest amount of crime involved physical violence with stealing in second place— both forms of aggression. Drunkenness, theft, assault, name calling or taunting were prevalent in this society and it did not make sense.

The reason why it didn't make sense and the problem for Bolton in evaluating this society was that the Qolla had no cultural memory of ever being like this prior to their encounter with western civilization. As Bolton noted in one of his papers on the Qolla, the old law of the Qolla was quite high in its standards for conduct: "In reality the Qolla do not have an ethic which extols violence or aggressiveness. Instead their moral code demands of them charity, compassion, and co-operation with all men." What's more, the villagers that Bolton interviewed extensively, reflected this in their speech and preached that goodness and charity were the duty of all men at all times. But as Bolton states, "the discrepancy between their own conduct and the conduct called for by the code . . . was enormous." The disparity could not be explained in conventional sociological terms, Bolton believed. There must be some other explanation.

What he did was synthesize several disciplines in his evaluation of this problem. Rather than relying on previous interpretations he combined a historical perspective along with sciences such as agriculture and medicine. The conclusion he reached was unique to anthropology and it raised a firestorm of controversy. It was very simple but precise, for all the facts of the matter fit into his model of interpretation rather elegantly. The social disturbances in the Qolla culture of Incawatana, Bolton theorized, were due to a severity of malnutrition— social mayhem due to consumption of partial-foods.

It was not that the Qolla had a lack of food to eat but it was, rather, *what* they ate that was causing the problem. Bolton synthesized the views of previous anthropologists while adding his own findings from agriculture and nutrition.

When the Qolla people were subjugated by the Inca and then the Western powers, a dramatic change occurred— their land was parceled out to them in meager amounts whereas, previous to this subjugation, they had much more access to fertile land. As a result of this partitioning, the land became overworked and depleted. The produce from the land became deficient in nutrients such as minerals and vitamin content. As Lee McDowell states in his book, *Minerals in Animal and Human Nutrition*, "Mineral deficiencies result most often when animals and humans are confined within a given area and are thus closely dependent upon the structure of the soil and the plant life in a very limited space. They no longer have recourse to migrations in order to compensate for the insufficiencies of the soil or the climate" (pg. 29) In this case the grains become only a source of sugar rather than a whole food which would have the vitamins and minerals along with the starch or sugar. In this depletion scenario you will have a disproportionate amount of sugar consumption. The food, though filling, is a depleted source of nutrients while only delivering sugar— hence, a partial-food, a counterfeit. This consumption of depleted food with only the sugars intact, according to Bolton, led to endemic hypoglycemia or chronic low blood sugar in the population. Hypoglycemia, in turn, is strongly implicated as a cause of social misbehavior including . . . crime.

Bolton put the theory to the test by administering a glucose tolerance test to the males of Incawatana. The results he got back proved his theory that hypoglycemia was correlated with aggression. He reported in his paper, *Aggression and Hypoglycemia in the Qolla* (Ethnology vol. 12, 1973), that "glucose homeostasis problems are widespread among the residents of Incawatana. Fully 55.5 percent of these men appear to have hypoglycemia . . ." Not only that but Bolton had the worst aggressors in Incawatana tested and he found that close to 90 percent of them were hypoglycemic— all due to partial-food consumption.

PRECURSORS TO SOCIAL DISORDER

Joseph Wilder, M.D., wrote and studied about this correlation between hypoglycemia (from partial-foods) and criminal behavior over 20 years before Bolton. In the medical field, Wilder noted that this concept between diet and social behavior was, at one time, anathema. In 1947 he wrote in *The Handbook of Correctional Psychology*: "Fifteen years ago it would have seemed preposterous to assume that there could be any relation between sugar metabolism and crime." To Wilder, the evidence was overwhelming as he catalogued various crimes that ranged from arson to homicide and mutilation which seemed to have a common denominator. All the criminals had hypoglycemia— a disordered sugar metabolism.

Even in Wilder's time the resistance to this correlation between hypoglycemia and crime was great. The establishment was not about to concede to the 'diet hypothesis' when it came to mental illness; much less would it concede to it when it came to social ills like crime and theft and juvenile delinquency.

Among other professional journals he also published his findings in the journal, *The Nervous Child* of 1944 volume 3 in an article entitled *Malnutrition and Mental Deficiency*. Here is what Wilder saw when children were hypoglycemic: "The child may be neurotic, psychopathic or have criminal tendencies and be subject to anxiety, running away tendencies, aggressiveness, a blind urge to activity and destructiveness, with impairment of moral sensibilities like shame." But this poor nutrition which is the cause of hypoglycemia can escalate the actions of a child or individual in a sociopathic direction: ". . . a considerable number of criminal and semi-criminal acts have been observed in children in hypoglycaemic (low blood sugar) states, ranging from destructiveness or violation of traffic regulations all the way to bestiality, arson and homicide."

As we shall see, when it is recognized for what it is— a disordered sugar metabolism due to partial-food consumption— and treated as such, the symptoms of the 'nervous child' or hyperactive child or ADHD child— go away.

Partial-foods equal hypoglycemia which equals negative behavioral change. The situation gets reversed when you re-introduce whole food.

THE SOLUTION

In the early 1970's, when the police Superintendent of Shipley, England, decided to do something about his 10 worst juvenile offenders, eyebrows were raised. These children were labeled as hyper-kinetic (every generation has their own label). The average arrest rate for these juveniles was more than once per month with their crimes ranging from violent assault, property damage, arson and theft. Superintendent Bennett referred these 10 worst to Dr. L. M. McEwen and his coworkers for study and possible help by changing their diets at home.

The diet consisted of two meats (e.g., lamb and chicken), two carbohydrate sources (e.g.., potatoes and rice), two fruits (e.g., bananas and pears), vegetables (cabbage, sprouts, cauliflower, broccoli, cucumber, celery, carrots), and water. The rice was later removed due to an allergic reaction some of the teens had. All the children responded immediately to the diet; the behavioral change was dramatic. So much so, that it made the authors of the study declare that a change of diet would prevent the juveniles from being in the correction system. Also, Dr. McEwen made an association between low blood sugar and antisocial behavior: "the hyper-kinetic syndrome is associated with reduced blood flow and reduced glucose metabolism in the frontal lobes of the brain." In other words, anti-social acts due to glucose stasis issues— hypoglycemia. This came to be known as the Shipley Project. (*Nutrition Digest*, Volume 36, No. 2)

Even though the connection between hypoglycemia and mental disposition has been reported in the major professional journals the dismissal of the phenomenon goes on by the establishment. What the nay-sayers are overlooking is that hypoglycemia not only affects the brain short term but it also effects long term change because your brain becomes *restructured*. In neuroscience, the principle of *neuroplasticity* states that, over time, the brain can change its very structure due to its surrounding chemical environment. This change can affect behavior in either a subtle way or in an extreme manner as this chapter has demonstrated. There are and there have been those, however, that have given heed to the evidence of the connection between diet and criminal behavior even in the face of resistance and ignorance.

Barbara Reed felt that she had found something that helped human lives, so we can understand her passion as she explained her story before the U.S. Senate Select Committee on Nutrition and Human Needs (1977). She was eventually questioned by a Senator from Kansas, Robert Dole, who doubted her premise by asking, "I wonder how many of these success stories are because of diet and how many are because they may have been receiving special attention, because someone cared about their rehabilitation." The doubt may have been somewhat justifiable by those on the committee because of the sheer unconventionality of what Mrs. Reed was relating. But the disbelief was in the underlying premise that nutrition and criminal behavior are directly related.

You see, Mrs. Reed was the Chief Probation officer for Cuyahoga County in the state of Ohio. She decided to implement a different approach in rehabilitating convicts. She took 252 offenders in the county jail system "who required attention as to their diet and vitamin needs." As she said this you can picture the senators taken aback in surprise by someone bringing up 'vitamins' in relation to criminals— but nothing could prepare them for what they heard next from the lips of Mrs. Reed when she reported the results of this 'dietary attention'. She stated to the committee that, "we have not had one single person back in court for trouble who has maintained and stayed on the nutritional diet."(*Correctional Treatment* pg.207) Clearly, the treatment for convicts made an impression on this veteran of the correctional system who had even given her self-hood in trying to rehabilitate habitual criminals, "I have been in this field for 14 years. I was giving people a lot of loving attention before without nearly the results as now . . . . never before has the court had such a tool for working with the many ill people who find themselves in court. We wonder what the result would be if this method of treatment could also be applied to all those sentenced to jail." (*Back to Basics*, pamphlet by Barbara Reed Stitt)

The criminologist, Alexander Schauss, came by this knowledge through observation. While working with heroin addicts in Harlem he noticed a disparity between certain individuals in recovery. The individuals who had not only kicked the habit but also changed their eating habits to 'eat more healthy' were successful in staying away from narcotics while those who ate 'junk food' continued to use or would relapse into using narcotics. Again later, while working with a youth rehabilitation home in South Dakota he noticed a peculiar thing. In one home called, "Our Home" in Huron, South Dakota there was something different happening. The juveniles were staying an average of three months before being released whereas the average release time for the state of South Dakota was 18 months. The difference? At the group home named 'Our Home', "the juveniles had their own garden from which they ate, with fresh unprocessed vegetables. No refined sugar, coffee or tea was served, but the youths were allowed wholesome nutritious snacks whenever they wished." He further explored and researched this connection and one of the fruits of this research was the book, *Diet, Crime and Delinquency*. Schauss chronicles experiments where criminals were corrected not by use of psychotherapy or jail time but by reintroducing nutrients into their diet.

The evidence that good nutrition can correct or improve sociopathic behavior is abundant and Schauss catalogs some examples of this in his book. For instance, in 1973 at the Morris county Jail Rehabilitation Center in New Jersey, a group from several universities set up an 8 week trial for a 'diet-vitamin' program. It emphasized high protein foods and vitamin supplements. The results of the study were improved morale, mood and motivation. Another thing that was interesting was the inmates decreased their sugar intake *voluntarily*.

In 1979, at a correctional center in Seattle for the U.S. Navy, the prison administrator, "took measures beginning in 1978 to curtail the availability of refined carbohydrates . . . . white flour was replaced with whole wheat . . . . granulated sugar was removed from the confines . . . removal of all pastries, cakes, ice cream, soft drinks and Kool Aid." All the partialfoods were thrown out. One year later the warden wrote to his superiors in Washington: "Since this time the medical log shows that a definite decrease in the number of confinees at sick call and on medication has occurred, and that disciplinary reports are down 12 percent."

Schauss reports on a small group home in Fairmount, Illinois during the 1970's for delinquents called the Purple Heart Homestead. Tamara Youngman, the proprietor of the home, received numerous commendations from correctional administrators in the state for her success in working "with those youths who have most often been cast out of every known institution." What was the secret to her success? According to Schauss, "the diet and nutrition program is considered essential to the rehabilitation process." He further elaborates: "From the day they arrive, all youths are placed on a balanced, natural foods diet. This diet is complete in all essential and nonessential amino acids, vitamins and minerals . . . this diet produces a marked drop in aggressive behavior. Megavitamin therapy is used to correct any chemical imbalance from previous drug abuse."

So we see that partial-foods like refined sugar not only can cause mental problems but they affect actions and behavior. Psychologist Stephen R. Buchanan wrote a paper entitled *The Most Ubiquitous Toxin*–he was referring to refined sugar–in which he stated "children who overconsume refined sugar are likely to upset the homeostatic balance necessary for proper metabolism, leading to behavioral changes and clinical symptoms such as hyperkinesis."(*American Psychologist* vol. 39, no. 11, pp. 1327-1328, 1984)

Behavior problems are wide-spread, affecting children, teens, and adults. Behavioral problems can be, like the other problems, 'sub-clinical' in their manifestations. The extreme may be criminal behavior but, as Wilder found out, anti-social behavior has a spectrum of effects that range from low-level negative behaviors such as road rage and general irritability, to high-level ones such as extreme aggression and violence. Almost no one seems to be exempt in this affair. It's almost as if everyone is being poisoned.

What is going on here with all these behavior problems is excessive sugar consumption. If you've understood chapter two, sugar can also act as a pica source. Societal restraints and taboos may interfere with the person choosing the logical pica source, which would be tobacco. As was shown in chapter two, choosing sugar for a pica source is a slope that is far more slippery than the tobacco slope. And since the magic mineral is a bare residue in sugar, more of it must be consumed. This will speed up the inflammatory process and side effects like hypoglycemia will intensify which in turn will restructure the brain which in turn may restructure *behavior*— which may give birth to a society that is much like the Qolla people.

Much of modern societal behavior may really be nothing more than the situation of the Qolla people 'writ large.'

Right now cigarette smoking, or any pica resonse, should seem insignificant compared to the larger picture. If you criticize or take away, by government mandate or societal pressure, a nutritional source for an important mineral, even though it's a nonfood substance, then we are reviving the dark ages.

TOBACCO IS THE RIGHT CHOICE

Cigarette smoking, and pica in general, is a *corrective response* to inflammation caused by chronic nutrient deficiency and not something to be blamed as a bad habit *in vacuo*. It's a law of nature:

Where there's FIRE (inflammation), there's smoking . . . or some other form of pica.

The irony is that cigarette smoking is called one of the primary lifestyle problems in the world when in fact the finger should be pointed at partial-foods. The cause is, or should be, greater than the effect. The cause is special hunger.

If the body is left to choose on its own, without the impediments of societal pressure or of unavailability, the body will reorient to the most effective pica source known as tobacco. Why is this so?

There are two reasons.

1) Tobacco smoke has the most absorbable form of the magic mineral. It's actually an ingenious delivery system in that it bypasses all the possible impediments of the gastrointestinal tract.

2) Tobacco contains a second nutrient that is ancillary yet supportive of the magic mineral and its actions. We could even call this second nutrient the Magic Vitamin . . .

CHAPTER 4: THE UNVEILING OF A VITAMIN

Smokers stands at a precipice, chased by the relentless monster of cigarette cravings. Most jump into the safety-nets of various cessation modalities such as nicotine replacement, hypnosis, willpower and other such treatments. Yet these nets are flimsy and frail as most smokers already know. They break. And the smoker crashes hard only to start looking for another precarious safety-net to jump into.

But there is an altenative at the seemingly hopeless precipice. The smoker can become armed with the most deadly weapon known to humanity for destroying monsters, whatever they be: knowledge.

HIDING IN PLAIN SIGHT

In the last chapter, one vitamin seemed to keep popping up when it came to illnesses and their treatment. Whether it was a physical skin disorder (pellagra) or a mental illness (schizophrenia), vitamin B-3 (commonly known as niacin) deficiency was behind the problem. But it also served as the remedy when restored to an individuals diet.

Interestingly, the name niacin is a portmanteau, a blending of two or more words together. However, this portmanteau seems to be hiding a very important fact— the true name of vitamin B-3, which is *nicotinic acid*. What was the reason for this name veiling? In his textbook, *Nutritional Biochemistry of the Vitamins* (2003), David Bender sheds some light on the subject: "It was felt nicotinic acid was not a suitable name for a substance that was to be added to foods, both because of its phonetic and chemical relationship to nicotine . . . " (pg.202)

A chemical relationship to nicotine?

We'll get to that but first let's see how they hid that relationship— the *ni-* in niacin is taken from the first two letters in the word *ni*cotinic, while the *ac-* is from the first two letters of the word *ac*id and the *-in* is taken from the last two letters in the word vitam*in*. These letters from the three words *ni*cotinic *ac*id vitam*in* combine to make the word niacin.

What exactly about that chemical relationship is being concealed?

From the same textbook, Bender throws us a most fascinating nugget: "Niacin is unusual among the vitamins in that it was discovered as a chemical compound, *nicotinic acid produced by the oxidation of nicotine*, in 1867— long before there was any suspicion that it might have a role in nutrition." (italics mine, Bender pg. 200)

Nicotine, the substance found in cigarettes that we're all familiar with, is only a loss of an electron or two away from becoming the vitamin known as nicotinic acid or B-3, or the veiled name of niacin, whichever you prefer.

Nicotine can become a vitamin.

The big question is can this process of oxidation occur in the human body? Is it possible that as soon as you go puff-puff on that cigarette that nicotine enters the process of oxidation and, hence, conversion to nicotinic acid, a vitamin?

The chemists in the employ of at least one tobacco company were well aware of nicotine converting into vitamin B-3 (nicotinic acid)— as a substance that was measurable in the saliva of people who smoked. There is a sense of excitement at this finding because of the time period. You see, at this time (the early 1940's), it was becoming well established that B-3 deficiency was the reason for pellagra disease. It was speculated that advertising for cigarettes could promote this 'health aspect' of tobacco.

An astonishing memo regarding this discovery can be found archived at the website

www.industrydocumentslibrary.ucsf.edu/tobacco/

[For some reason or other the home web address for these documents changes. I don't know why this happens but since the last version of this book I know it has at least once. If it happens to change again you can email me at the address I've left at the beginning of the book and I'll be glad to forward the documents]

The website is a clearinghouse of documents that are organized and gathered due to the "Master Settlement Agreement between the States and the tobacco companies." As a result of this lawsuit "the industry was required to make the documents used during the trials available." This includes most every memo that was circulated within the various tobacco companies. You can do some homework if you want. If you go to the website address listed above, type the number 04365490 in the first search field. Then, in the second field which is entitled Search Options, select Tobacco Collections and then select 'Lorillard' ONLY (deselect the others) and then click on search. A page will come up that says Nicotinic acid— click on it and then scroll down to the bottom to look at the memo. What you will find is a 3 page memo from a chemist to an executive at the P. Lorrilard company in which the chemist has discovered, in his words, something "quite remarkable" and useful as "material for advertising purposes."

So what was this discovery that the chemists found "quite remarkable"? "We find that the smoke from ordinary Ripple cigarettes contains the anti-pellagra vitamin, or nicotinic acid, in fairly substantial amounts." The particular chemist writing this, representing his co-workers, goes on to say that, "we doubted that vitamins could be absorbed from tobacco smoke by the throat and lung tissues. However, we have now found that nicotinic acid is dissolved in the saliva of the smoker when smoking ordinary cigarettes . . . these conclusions are based on actual analyses of saliva, collected from a smoker while smoking . . ." It's safe to say that the excited chemist never got the approval for the further testing that he was requesting.

The conversion of nicotine into the vitaminic form of B-3 or nicotinic acid is a known fact amongst chemists— outside of the body. The professional publication known as *Organic Syntheses,* in its own words, since 1921 has "provided the chemistry community with detailed, reliable, and carefully checked procedures for the synthesis of organic compounds." One of these procedures that is detailed is the conversion of nicotine into nicotinic acid— vitamin B-3. In *Organic Syntheses,* Collective Volume 1, (1945) the authors state, "Nicotinic acid can be prepared by oxidation of nicotine with nitric acid, potassium permanganate or chromic acid . . ."

It's a scientific, hard fact. Nicotine, when oxidized, turns into nicotinic acid. Can this occur inside the human body?

IF IT WALKS AND TALKS LIKE A DUCK

If nicotine converts into nicotinic acid in the body then we should be able to find studies that show congruence between the two in their effects. In other words, nicotine will show itself to *act* quite like nicotinic acid, physiologically.

If this is found to be true then we could say that, in a sense, nicotine is a "pre-vitamin".

The strange fact is that there are hardly any studies to demonstrate what nicotine metabolizes into outside the liver (extra-hepatically). The liver and kidneys is where the focus is concerning metabolization of nicotine, as it normally should be, but shouldn't we be including what's going on in the brain? Why the exclusive focus on the liver and kidneys for a pharmacological substance that we know affects the brain and is supposedly an addictive substance? It seems a bit odd but it's true. In a scientific paper reviewing the literature on nicotine metabolization the authors admit that there is a scarcity of research in brain metabolization of nicotine: "Extrahepatic nicotine metabolism clearly needs more research in humans." (Pharmacological Reviews March 2005 vol. 57 no. 1 79-115).

So if the conjecture is right, that nicotine morphs into nicotinic acid (vitamin B3), then studies will show exact similarities in their physiological effects. Here are just a few examples:

Nicotine stimulates dopamine levels in the brain. This is a well established fact (*Journal of Pharmacology and Experimental Therapeutics* 2000 Aug;294(2):458-65). Not only that but it seems to extend the half life of dopamine by preventing its destruction.

But what about nicotinic acid or vitamin B-3? It turns out that NAD(H), the nicotinic acid based co-enzyme, also stimulates dopamine levels in the brain (*Biochimica et Biophysica acta* 1997 Jul 10;1361(1):59-65).

Nicotine raises blood sugar *(Medecine Interne* 1980 Oct-Dec;18(4):353-6).

And, as you can guess, nicotinic acid (niacin or vitamin B-3) also raises blood sugar. (Clofibrate and niacin in coronary disease. JAMA 1975; 231: 360-381)

Nicotine stimulates growth hormone (*Psychopharmacology* December 1982, Volume 78, Issue 4, pp 305-308).

Nicotinic acid also stimulates growth hormone (Society for Experimental Biology and Medicine 1967 126:708).

Nicotine promotes the growth of new blood vessels known as angiogenesis. The study, initially published in the July, 2001 issue of Nature Medicine, was summarized and subsequently reported in various online and print science news outlets. The study that demonstrated this took place at the Stanford University Medical Center. According to ScienceDaily.com July 31, 2001, "The researchers were somewhat surprised to find how strongly nicotine stimulates new blood vessel growth, a process known as angiogenesis." One of the researchers stated that the exact opposite was expected of nicotine: "We expected to see that nicotine impairs angiogenesis because it's known that smoking impairs endothelial function." The study suggests that "nicotine treatment may be useful to revive tissue deprived of blood by a stroke or heart attack."

And it shouldn't come as a surprise that niacin also stimulates new blood vessels (*Annals of Neurology* (Impact Factor 11:19 06/2007; 62(1):49 - 58 published by Wiley and the American Neurological Association).

Nicotine has been shown to have an anxiolytic effect (*Phar-

macology, Biochemistry and Behavior 2001 Jul-Aug;69(3-4):511-8). Smokers know this anecdotally when they smoke a cigarette to relax or 'calm down', for instance.

But niacin has also been shown to be an anti-anxiety nutrient in the laboratory (*Science* 18 January 1980: Vol. 207 no. 4428 pp. 274-281).

The following is just one of many summations from the scientific community extolling the benefits of nicotine. From the *British Journal of Addiction* in its May 1991 issue: "When chronically taken, nicotine may result in: (1) positive reinforcement, (2) negative reinforcement, (3) reduction of body weight, (4) enhancement of performance, and protection against; (5) Parkinson's disease (6) Tourette's disease (7) Alzheimers disease, (8) ulcerative colitis and (9) sleep apnea. The reliability of these effects varies greatly but justifies the search for more therapeutic applications for this interesting compound."(British Journal of Addiction 1991 May;86(5):571-5)

And, quite conveniently, niacin is instrumental in all of the above. Niacin is vital in weight loss and it enhances performance. It has been shown through various studies that niacin protects against Parkinson's, Tourette's, Alzheimer's, ulcerative colitis, and it helps people with sleep disorders.

Niacin and nicotine seem to be interchangeable as far as their effects physiologically. Can this be dismissed as mere mimicry or are they really the same thing because nicotine is getting oxidized into nicotinic acid? But even if this oxidation of nicotine is not occurring in the human body the data shows that vitamin B3 is one of the substances that is found in actual tobacco smoke. This is what the chemists from Lorillard may have run into. The textbook *Chemical Components of Tobacco and To-*

bacco Smoke is a compendium of practically every study ever done that analyzed the substances that are in tobacco and in the actual smoke. In the thirteenth chapter of this textbook we read the following: "In their 1959 review of tobacco and tobacco smoke components, Johnstone and Plimmer described the identification of asparagine and glutamine in tobacco and glutamine and nicotinamide in tobacco smoke."

Did you get that last part? Not only has an amino acid, such as glutamine, been found in tobacco smoke but a vitamin known as nicotinamide, otherwise known as vitamin B3, has also been identified and verified. In the actual smoke!

Either way (whether oxidation occurs in the body at some point or tobacco smoke just naturally contains B3) the fact of the matter is that tobacco delivers a vitamin that happens to be essential in many cellular functions. The body is making an intelligent choice by selecting a vitamin that bypasses the gastrointestinal tract, with all its potential problems of absorption, and becomes readily absorbed and used by the brain.

The smoker is not addicted to nicotine, he is starving for it.

ENRICHING DOESN'T SOLVE THE PROBLEM

Since the early 1940's the government of the United States prodded food companies into putting the B vitamins back into refined grain end-products because there was a definite awareness of what vitamin B deficiency could do to a population, as was evidenced with the beriberi outbreak and pellagra. The food companies, through the 'nudging' of the government and pressure from health advocates, eventually addressed the problem.

They added the essential B vitamins, that they stripped out through refining, in synthetic form. These were not natural in any way but synthesized in a laboratory. This is a process that continues to this day. The grain end-products are called 'enriched' as a result of this process.

An example of this attempt to put back in what the food manufacturers originally pillaged is a slogan from a bread company used during the 1950's: "Helps build bodies 12 different ways." What was this slogan referring to? The claim was to lessen the public's fear that these grain end-products were dangerous because they were stripped of valuable vitamins. This slogan was, in a sense, saying "Hey, we put back 12 of these nutrients back into the product . . . so you don't have to worry."

But what isn't readily shared with the populace is that the refining process takes out far more than twelve nutrients. It is estimated that over twenty five nutrients are taken out of cereal grains by the refining process. By saying that a fraction of the amount is put back in by 'enriching' the product does not make it a whole food again. The problem gets even worse when adjuncts like refined sugar are added to these products— and they inevitably always are.

The B vitamins added back in are always laboratory-made vitamins. There is good evidence that these synthetic vitamins are not the ideal form for human consumption and absorption. They do not have the same efficacy as a naturally derived vitamin in a biological system such as the human body. Dr. Szent Gyiorgi, who discovered ascorbic acid, realized this in his laboratory studies in the 1930's. He published his findings in the journal *Nature* (July 1936, 138, 27-4) in a paper entitled *Vitamin P: Flavonols as vitamins*. Here is the big point of the study: He realized that there was more to vitamin C than just, simply, ascorbic acid. Ascorbic acid seemed to be part of a greater complex which comprised the C vitamin. Ascorbic acid can be made in a laboratory but the whole complex cannot be duplicated in a lab the way it is in nature. And the most important thing he found was that the natural vitamin was much more effective in treating patients than the synthetic ascorbic acid.

So even though the B family is added back into the product it is not as nutritionaly effective as the natural state of the vitamin. In other words, even though you are eating a product that is enriched with niacin your body may still be starving for it. It will not be as physiologically effective in preventing the flames of inflammation.

Conclusion: You are still starving for niacin

Perhaps you think that you are reasonably supplementing your diet with a multi-vitamin or some other supplement that contains the B vitamins in a natural form. This is great but it won't solve the problem of niacin deficiency if you have refined sugar in your diet throughout the day. If you add niacin to your diet and you consume a good amount of refined sugar in snacks, pastries, etc., your supplementing with B vitamins can never be commensurate due to the *concentration* of sugar.

Here's what I mean. Whenever you concentrate a product, such as cane sugar when it is refined, that concentration amount represents a far greater amount of *whole* food and the great amount of nutrients in that same whole food. However, those nutrients which are necessary in metabolizing the sugar, are gone. For example, let's say that you drink a can of soda or say, even, a so-called 'energy' drink each day. If there are 39 grams of refined sugar in a 12 ounce can of soda how many sugar cane plants must be consumed to equal this one can of soda to obtain the nutrients that are necessary for that sugar to be metabolized? Approximately 30 cane stalks which are over six feet tall. Remember, the sugar cane plant will, in addition to sugar, have the necessary vitamins and minerals to metabolize the sugar in it but a concentration has nothing of the sort. In order to metabolize those 39 grams you would need all the vitamins and minerals that are stripped away from those 30 plus stalks that are over six feet tall. Not even taking a mega-vitamin supplement could keep up with that pace.

But this is exactly what is happening in a partial-food diet—the required nutrients for metabolization are missing.

Conclusion: You are still starving for niacin

So, even though a product may claim to be 'enriched', it is still not giving you all the other factors needed to metabolize that added sugar. Even if niacin is added to the product (what is known as *enriching*) it can not equal the amount needed to metabolize the *concentrated* product.

You'll be starving for a primary nutrient. When the body reorients toward tobacco it does so to fulfill a nutritional need. Tobacco can readily supply this nutrient in the form of nicotine.

TWO PIECES TO THE PUZZLE

Is niacin via nicotine the missing nutrient the smoker is searching for? In other words, if you were to put niacin back into your diet, in the right amounts, would the desire to smoke completely vanish? To some extent it would . . . but not completely. If you supplement only with niacin you will notice a slight diminishment in your cravings. I tried this on myself a few times and I went from smoking 20 cigarettes a day to about 12 to 15 or so a day. Is that a big change? Not really. I've known a handful of people that cut their cigarette habit in half by taking niacin throughout the day. Just niacin, no magic mineral. On average, taking niacin alone can cut your cigarette intake from 1/4 to 1/3.

Niacin alone can not completely eliminate your cravings. There is another factor in tobacco that is even more important which happens to have a synergistic relationship with niacin.

Nicotine is only part of the equation of why people need to smoke.

There are now researchers who are looking at the evidence on nicotine addiction and find it completely lacking. Professor Peter Killeen of Arizona State University presented his research findings for the National Institute on Drug Abuse, in a talk entitled, "Reefer Madness: There Ain't No Such Thing as Addiction to Nicotine." His research brought him to some conclusions that were somewhat contrary to the academic and public opinion on the matter.

"I came up with a shocking discovery," Killeen said. "There's no such thing as nicotine addiction." He also stated the now obvious conclusion of many studies: "Studies have shown that none of the nicotine replacement therapies — chewing gum, inhalers, patches — none of those are addictive. Nicotine is not addictive. So what's going on?" Killeen believes that there is some other factor involved in smoking addiction. He believes that nicotine is involved with some other chemical in the cigarette that creates the 'need' to smoke; he calls it a sort of 'nicotine cocktail' which gives the cigarette a 'one-two punch' to the brain. He also expressed that if this is not recognized widely, (the fact that nicotine is not addictive), then the answer to smoking addiction will not be found: "Not everybody knows that nicotine is not addictive. This negatively affects both the research and public opinion."

Killeen was only reporting on the research. In NIDA Notes (Volume 13, Number 3 July, 1998), a publication of the National Institute of Drug Abuse, we see a title that reflects this research years before Killeen made his speech: "Tobacco Smoke May Contain a Psychoactive Ingredient Other Than Nicotine", reads the headline.

In 2014 Dr. Paul Newhouse, the director of Vanderbilt University's Center for Cognitive Medicine, stated in an interview, concerning nicotine studies that he performed, that, "There were no addiction or withdrawal problems, and nobody started smoking cigarettes. The risk of addiction to nicotine alone is virtually nil." This is the same conclusion that Killeen came to after looking at various studies. There simply is no addiction factor in nicotine. Newhouse, in the same interview, says, "Nicotine is not reinforcing enough. That's why FDA agreed nicotine could be sold over the counter. No one wants to take it because it's not pleasant enough by itself. And it's hard to get animals to self-administer nicotine the way they will with cocaine."

It boils down to this. People trying to quit are not dying to have a nicotine patch or craving nicotine gum. Nobody craves these things with the same intensity that they do the cigarette. No one craves nicotine on its own.

Killeen and Newhouse realize that there is something else going on with cigarette smokers. There is another factor involved in so-called cigarette addiction. Combined with nicotine, this element forms the 'one-two punch' that Killeen talked about. As you will discover after reading the next chapter, when this element is offered to the body in the form of food and/or supplement, in the right amounts, the desire for smoking vanishes.

Nicotinic acid (vitamin B-3) is the smaller (yet still important) part of the puzzle.

The most important piece of the puzzle in the smoking conundrum is a mineral.

CHAPTER 5: THE MAGIC MINERAL

There's a very old story that tells us our material aspect was derived from the " dust of the ground." With the benefit of modern science we know today that the lithosphere of the earth, the " dust of the ground" referred to in this story, is composed of minerals. But what is remarkable is how many of these minerals of the "dust from the ground" have physiological functions in the human body. Without minerals, enzymatic reactions cannot occur efficiently in the cellular environment.

And if there are no enzymatic reactions there will be no life.

Plants take these minerals and wrap them up into their very structure. In turn, these plants become mineral sources for animals. And then these animals and plants become mineral sources when they are eaten by humans. Hence, the dust of the earth, the minerals and elements, become incorporated into the very structure and function of the human body through this Great Cycle of life.

However, the Great Cycle can be interrupted by the machinations of humans. If humans take plants and remove the mineral content from their end-products through refining methods, this removes the life giving force of the plant. When this happens a most peculiar phenomenon will take place. Men and women will turn to and consume the dust of the earth (see chapter two) because he/she needs the most important element that the dust contains. As has been shown in the first few chapters, this is the pica response, and it has many forms but the main goal of this response is to obtain the Magic Mineral, which happens to be the most abundant element of the earth's crust besides oxygen.

It is this element that man is trying to incorporate into his being when he engages in pica by consuming nonfoods such as clay and tobacco. The nonfoods act as carriers of this most important element. This principle is universal. For dust we are and it is dust (minerals) that we must consume to live. And the dust of the earth is mainly (besides oxygen) composed of the magic mineral— the element known as silicon.

The deficiency of this mineral is the reason you smoke.

THE SHADOWY MINERAL

Silicon, as we shall see later, is hardly found by itself— it is a *lover of oxygen* and always found bound with it. Because of this the general term used for it is silicon dioxide or commonly referred to as silica. On earth, oxygen is the most common element and it is pretty important in terms of human functioning. Most everyone understands this— if you have no oxygen you die. However, even though the second most abundant element in the crust is silica, there is almost complete ignorance and negligence concerning its function in human physiology. But the studies that are being done point to silica as not only fundamental in structural formation of the human skeleton but also in cellular processes and even brain function.

The French scientist Louis Kevran discovered a highly controversial (at the time) property of silica in the 1960's. The reason it was so controversial, until the last few years, can best be demonstrated by a simple question: What is the most important mineral for bone growth and structure? Most scientists, nutritionists, doctors and even your friends would say, undoubtedly, that it is calcium that is most important. It was most astounding then when Kevran found that it was actually silica that stimulated growth in bone fractures and not calcium. "Calcium," he states, "has never been found to enter into the bones." (*Biological Transmutations* pg. 74) Silica seems to form a matrix on which calcium is laid. Without the matrix or structure that silica forms, calcium can not be deposited. Though Kevran and others like Dr. Pierre Delbet discovered these properties of silica over 50 years ago the rest of the world ignored the findings.

Until now. As recently as February 2004 a study published in the *Journal of Bone and Mineral Research* stated at the outset regarding silica, that "its contribution to bone health is not known." In other words, for years scientists ignored Kevran's claims. But after the study was done the authors realized that silica *was* indeed critical to bone health. "Higher dietary silicon intake in men and younger women may have salutary effects on skeletal health, especially cortical bone health, *that has not been previously recognized.*" (my italics) This study had close to 3,000 participants ranging from age to 30 to 87.

This property of structural formation that silica has is even seen in more supple organs and body parts such as the vascular system. The arteries are virtual deposits of silica, especially the aorta. Kevran also anticipated these findings by at least 20 years. A study published in the journal *Atherosclerosis* in 1979 by Loeper and Loeper found that silica "inhibits experimental atheromas normally induced by an atheromatous diet, making atheromatous plaques much rarer and lipid deposits more superficial." The authors of the report called silica 'antiatheromatous'. An atheroma is a type of swelling or plaque that is implicated in clogging of the arteries. What is also interesting about this, however, is that the researchers were puzzled by the mechanism of how silica accomplishes this by stating that the "mechanism of silicon's antiatheromatous action remains *shadowy*." (italics mine)

This seems to be the conclusion in mainstream science about silica— that it is somewhat of a puzzle, that it lurks in the backround yet quietly exhibits astounding qualities. The scientific establishment has yet to see what greater implications this mineral has in metabolic function of the human organism and cell.

THE SILICA PLANT

Tobacco is a silicon accumulator. It absorbs silicon from the soil and then incorporates it into its structure. However, tobacco is not the highest silicon accumulator in the plant kingdom; there are other plants that have a greater affinity for silicon from the soil. So why do humans choose this plant as a pica source? The delivery system known as smoking, is the most potent form of silica transmission to the brain. It is simple to understand this. Smoking bypasses the gastro-intestinal system of the human body and all the possible barriers that that system could have in absorbing a nutrient. The result is silica in a highly absorbable form.

Even though it is not the highest silicon accumulator in the plant kingdom, tobacco does have a good amount in the form of phytoliths. Dental researchers noted this when they were trying to figure out the puzzle of tooth wear that was occurring in people who chewed tobacco exclusively rather than smoking it. The puzzle was that the teeth of these people looked as if they had been chewing on a hard object such as rocks or gravel, such was the wear of their teeth. The relatively soft texture of chewing tobacco did not match the profile of what was being done to their teeth. How could chewing tobacco accomplish this? After subjecting the tobacco leaves to an acid bath the mineral residue exposed what was causing the problem. Though they were minute particles (50 to 500 microns), it was found that they were composed of silica and silica compounds. The researchers were careful to exclude any contaminants or dirt that may have been left on leaves, so they submitted the leaves to a rigorous cleaning that included soft bristle brushing and ultrasonic vibration. They took a closer look at the leaves under a microscope and here is what they found regarding silica: "Examination of the tobacco leaves under a dissecting microscope (x32) revealed particles embedded in the surface, despite previous ultrasonic and mechanical removal of surface dust." They concluded that these particles of silica must be a "part of the leaf structure as the result of metabolic processes of the plant itself." (*Journal of the American Dental Association* March 1995)

What you will find in chapter eight is that this finding was not (and is not) news to certain American Indian tribes. As we'll see later, the ancient American Indians had long known that the tobacco plant was related to a rock. In one of their legends they call tobacco a brother to a 'rock', namely quartz. And what is quartz? Crystalline structure of silicon dioxide.

A LOVE AFFAIR

We have noted, so far, the structural importance of silica but there is a far greater thing that silica does for the body, and the brain in particular, and it has to do with silica's *function*. Silica is the greatest natural anti-inflammatory known to man because silica puts out the *fire in the brain.*

The reason for silica's impressive ability to stamp out inflammation is because of its two affinities— silica has a love affair with two substances. The love affair is with:

1) Oxygen and
2) Water

And these two substances compose the primary matrix in which our cells operate and, by extension, the whole human organism. That is, they not only have a primary role in eliminating inflammation but they are that through which and by which normal physiological processes are able to occur. And silica is the physiological *manager* of these two, especially in the brain. The smoker is correctly following his instinct which, really, is a hunger response. For if this natural anti-inflammatory and equalizer of environment (through its management of water and oxygen) is missing in the food supply, the body will reorient itself to obtain this fire fighter in nonfood forms such as tobacco. To disobey this inclination would be a foolish act, and hubris defined, for it is the natural wisdom of the body that is being expressed when a smoker desires tobacco. To fight it is to fight gravity.

If one grasps this principle one can easily detect the remedy to this situation. All one needs to do is supply this mineral in the diet, through food and/or supplement form, in the right amounts and the reorientation toward nonfoods will stop. In other words, if your pica response happens to be smoking, all desires and cravings will vanish once you put this mineral back into your diet. You are merely restoring what has been removed from the food supply.

Before we get on to silica's attraction to oxygen and water we must address a huge error in thinking that has been propagated to the ends of the earth. It has to do with the anti-oxidant/free radicals theory of disease and aging. In short, oxygen can be a bad guy in a cellular environment when it interacts with certain other chemicals. This interaction then causes a thing known as free radicals which cause harm and what we need is to buffer this process by consuming nutrients that are called anti-oxidants.

Oxygen is not the bad guy. Let's use a little analogy: If a restaurant owner carelessly dumps his garbage outside, why should he blame the congregation of rats around his business? The rats are not the problem here, they're only doing their job as scavengers. In the same way, oxygen only causes problems when there is an already underlying state of decomposition of matter. When something is in a state of decay oxygen interacts and thus begins what could be called oxidative damage. Oxygen does not initialize the condition of decay but it does enhance it and bring it to completion. When you're alive you don't find your body decomposing from oxygen as it would when you are dead. Once something is dead, or beginning to decay, oxygen begins to do its rightful job as scavenger and enhances the process of breaking down matter. Once again, oxygen attacks something that is dead or in the stages of dying. The term anti-oxidant is a huge misnomer. The problem is not oxygen but an underlying system of decay that is occurring at the cellular level. The underlying problem is actually an overly-acidic cellular environment, otherwise known as inflammation . . . which silica balances out because one of its love affairs is with water. It's real simple. If you want to neutralize something overly acidic, just pour some water into it. And silica helps in doing just that.

That silica is a water lover can be shown in a simple way by observing something in daily life. Commercially, silica has numerous uses but the one we may be familiar with is those silica gel packets that are put into vitamin jars and various other items. The reason why is that the silica packet absorbs any surrounding moisture in order to inhibit mold growth. Silica has an incredible hygroscopic ability— the ability to attract and hold water molecules from the surrounding environment. Though this is for water in a gaseous form (water vapor) there is evidence that silicon does this for water in its liquid form. Now, this is all well and good for there are other elements that have this property with water but there is something strange and different about silica. It seems to have an added dimension to it that other hygroscopic elements are lacking.

Not only is it a water attractor but silica seems to be a *water manager*. This has readily been demonstrated in many studies throughout the world involving plants. If a plant is slightly dehydrated and silica is made available to a plant for uptake, silica will ensure the plant gets its water. On the other hand, if the plant has too much water, silica will balance this out by not taking in any more. It seems to equalize the hydration of living things. In various studies whenever silica is available to the plant, inevitably, the biomass of the plant increases. In botany they refer to this as 'fresh weight. This fresh weight is interesting because it is not only strictly water but also the inclusion of solids which contribute to overall plant structure and rigidity and function. Silica seems to be acting as some sort of attractor for much needed nutrients.

The biggest stressor of plants worldwide is salt. Excessive salt draws in too much water, thereby damaging the plant. Silica is able to somehow deter salt so that the plant does not absorb as much water. Time and again, in the laboratory, when plants are subjected to 'salt stress' the plants that have silica available to them are always able to repel the problem by mobilizing built in defense mechanisms, which include enzymes like peroxidase and super-oxide dismutase, to a greater degree than plants that have silica withheld from them. The plants with silica available to them "rebound" quicker in these situations.

Sodium (nor other minerals) does not seem to have the two way management capacity for water that silica does. Silica is able to attract water but also, even in the presence of salt, to repel water. It keeps an equilibrium in the environment or, one might say, *silica initiates and encourages homeostasis.*

Why is this important as it pertains to humans or specifically the habit known as smoking? Remember, silica is in tobacco in the form of phytoliths which are embedded in the leaf. When an individual smokes he is absorbing silica in a dissolved, particulate form. Though this form of silica intake may be transient (i.e. it is only momentary and not "layed down" into structure) the smoker is still taking in a regulator, a stabilizer of sorts, which mitigates against inflammation in the internal environment of the brain.

THE BRAIN IS A SILICON CHIP

Though silica is a part of every structure in the body it was the scientist, Edith Carlyle, who pointed out and distinguished its primary importance in the brain. In the text *Silicon Biochemistry* she noted that certain areas of the rat brain have a higher degree of silicon concentration than other areas from dietary uptake. According to scientists rodent brains are very similar to human brains in function and anatomy. The entire set-up of the brain is nearly identical. Both use the same neurotransmitters and receptors, the same proteins for synaptic vesicle release and recycling, and similar signaling mechanisms. Knowing this, let's get back to what Carlyle discovered. She states, "regional concentrations of silicon varied. For instance, in the hippocampus, caudate and lentiform nucleus, silicon concentrations were greater than in the other nine regions examined. It appeared as if silicon had some function in the brain."(pg.176) These last words are quite interesting. She felt that the different concentration levels implied functionality; the same type of reasoning we would use for the rest of the body.

The interesting thing is where Carlyle noted the silica is concentrated. For instance, the hippocampus is established as one of the main places where our memories are stored and formed. In Alzheimer patients the hippocampus is one of the first areas to show degeneration. Could it be that the silica, which is a structural part of the hippocampus, is being depleted?

There was a study in France that was published in the *American Journal of Clinical Nutrition* (2005;81:897–902) in which silica intake played a primary role in cognitive behavior. Close to 8,000 French women over the age of 75 years old participated. At the beginning of the study the women were assessed as to how much silica was being taken in their diet and then tests were given. Dr. Allen Gaby writes, "Women with lower intakes of silica were found to perform worse on cognitive function tests, compared with women whose silica intake from drinking water was higher."

Follow ups were done on some of the women for up to seven years and Gaby concluded that, "During the follow-up period, women with lower intake of silica were at increased risk of developing Alzheimer's disease; those who developed Alzheimer's disease were nearly three times as likely to have a low silica intake from drinking water (4 mg per day or less)."

So it should not be surprising if tobacco use is reported as having a protective effect in Alzheimer's disease or in any form of dementia. This is precisely the case as study after study confirmed the association between smoking and positive brain health. From this sampling of reports one thing should be emphasized and that is the diversity of the sources. From the *International Journal of Epidemiology*, 1991: "A statistically significant inverse association between smoking and Alzheimer's disease was observed at all levels of analysis, with a trend towards decreasing risk with increasing consumption." The *British Medical Journal* reported in June 22, 1991, that "The risk of Alzheimer's disease decreased with increasing daily number of cigarettes smoked before onset of disease. . . ."

MUDDY WATERS

In order for neurotransmitters to function properly they must have an environment conducive to jumping the gap of the neuronal synapse. If the surrounding environment is too "acidic" the neurotransmitters are "stuck in a swamp" that is difficult to cross, so to speak. The brain even has special sensors that are specifically designed to watch out for this type of situation. These sensors have only one function and that is to monitor the acidity levels of the blood. They are simply known as *acid sensing ion channels* or ASICS. These channels monitor the pH levels of the blood throughout the central nervous system. Again, they are highly sensitive to hydrogen which in turn is an indicator of the acidity of the environment.

Silica will prevent this build up to acidosis in the brain environment because it is an attractor of water and oxygen. These two must be available in the brain environment in the right proportions in order for neurotransmitters to fire across the gap. They are the boat and oars which are necessary for the neurotransmitters to be carried across the synapse. But if silica is not available the brain invokes another management system which is not as efficient.

If there is not sufficient water and oxygen–the acidity levels are high–the neurotransmitters will invoke emergency measures to 'jump the gap', which they must do in order to maintain brain function. Keep in mind, this secondary management system is not the ideal.

This fall-back emergency system involves calcium and certain enzymes. We could call it the calcium/enzyme system. More calcium than usual is called upon to jump the gap when silica is not available. Calcium has the ability to create a pressure that will overcome the membrane potential of any cell, even in an extreme acidosis environment— it forces the situation. There is an urgency in this action of calcium because if transmitters do not fire we have the brain coming to a halt; otherwise known as death. However, additional calcium is not the best boat for the neurotransmitters to cross on.

Calcium does not have the management ability of silica. It only acts in one direction. It has a single minded zeal that goes a little too far unless something else comes in to stop it from going overboard. Because it is so good at what it does we now have the reverse of the original problem. With additional calcium the neurotranmitters will now over-fire so we now have the problem of too many neurotransmitters in the gap. The brain will not allow this hyperpolarization to occur because this too can mean death so it will put a halt to calcium's one way thinking by using certain enzymes to degrade or break down the excess neurotransmitters. These enzymes act as a sort of 'brake' to calciums over-firing excesses. The names of these 'brakes' are monoamine oxidase A and monoamine oxidase B (MAO A and MAO B). There is an antagonistic battle occurring here of 1) more calcium being called upon to initiate neurotransmitter release because the environment is too acidic (inflammation) but then 2) this action having to be reversed or mitigated somewhat by the monoamine oxidase enzymes because there are too many transmitters now. In the journal known as *BMC Neuroscience* (2007 8:73), a study entitled *Calcium-sensitive regulation of monoamine oxidase-A contributes to the production of peroxyradicals in hippocampal cultures*, demonstrates that calcium and the MAO enzymes work together— but not very efficiently. According to the scientists, whenever calcium levels rise there seems to be an increase in at least one of the MAO enzymes: "Calcium (Ca^{2+}) has recently been shown to selectively increase the activity of monoamine oxidase-A (MAO-A) . . . It has also been suggested that increased intracellular free Ca^{2+} levels as well as MAO-A may be contributing to the oxidative stress associated with Alzheimer disease (AD)." Translation? Too much acidity, or inflammation, because the brain is on the secondary, fall-back emergency calcium/enzyme system because the supreme water manager known as silica is missing in the diet.

This constant tug of war of the secondary management system will always occur if a person is deprived of the natural management system which involves silica and vitamin B-3, nicotinic acid.

So . . . if you goad someone into stopping smoking or take cigarettes away from a person without replacing silica and B-3 in some form, there will be damage done in both the physical and, as a result, the psychic realm. In the psychiatric field the monoamine oxidase enzymes have been implicated in depression. There seems to be a high correlation between the depressed state and high amounts of these enzymes. In other words, if an individual is depressed there's a good chance that he has high amounts (or higher than normal) of monoamine oxidase enzymes in his system. A person suffering from depression is on the secondary management system which is a poor one compared to the ideal— silica and vitamin B-3. So, as you may have guessed already, the MAO enzymes, which are a part of the secondary management system and also associated with depression, are practically non-existent in smokers . . .

In the January 2003 issue of the journal *Neurotoxicology* the researchers admit "Current cigarette smokers have reduced monoamine oxidase (MAO) and there is evidence that this is a pharmacological effect of tobacco smoke exposure rather than a biological characteristic of smokers." Other studies reflect the same opinion such as the one published in the journal known as *PNAS* (Proceedings of the National Academy of Sciences) in November of 1996. The researchers concluded that "Our results show that tobacco smoke exposure is associated with a marked reduction in brain MAO A."

In essence, the MAO enzymes are vacuum cleaners that pick up 'junk' neurotransmitters that are doing nothing, that are left in the synaptic gap between neurons, just lazing about. The MAO enzymes dispose of leftovers, of garbage. So if you have high levels of these MAO enzymes it means one thing: You have a lot of junk in your brain. This is the reason that researchers are eyeing MAO enzymes as the cause of depression.

Once again, smokers do not have high levels of these junk cleaners because there is no junk there or minimal junk to clean up. Why?

Again, this is all very simple. Smokers are being supplied with the two main nutrients of brain function: vitamin B-3 and, most importantly, silica. They are not on the emergency management system which involves additional calcium and the MAO enzymes. Therefore the MAO enzymes will be virtually nonexistent in smokers. Now, if these two nutrients are restored in the diet, you will not have the cravings to smoke and the brain will not have to resort to this emergency management system.

THE ONE - TWO PUNCH

Researchers have known for quite some time that nicotine is acting along with something else . . . nicotine is not the so-called "addictive" substance as Peter Killeen concluded (chapter 4). In the *Journal of Neuroscience* (Monoamine Oxidase Inhibition Dramatically Increases the Motivation to Self-Administer Nicotine in Rats September 21, 2005) the authors of this study state that "Nicotine is not the only compound in tobacco. There are over 4000 chemical constituents in tobaccco smoke, some of which have pharmacological effects and thus may contribute to tobacco dependence." There may be other compounds that are the cause of tobacco dependence? This piece of news hasn't hit the newstands or the five o'clock news yet I'm sure. But why are these scientists saying this? According to these researchers, "Nicotine has relatively weak reinforcing properties compared with other drugs. Such a weak reinforcing property cannot explain by itself the intense addictive properties of tobacco smoking, the difficulty most smokers experience in attempting to quit, and the high relapse rates after quitting." It may not be on the headline news but this is what the research is showing.

Nicotine is not the only substance doing something in the brain. The main substance is silica because it is causing a clean environment for neurotransmitters to do their jobs. In fact, both substances are neuroprotective in that they provide a "clean" environment for the brain to operate.

Silica and B-3 show these characteristics individually in studies. In other words when they isolate either one, silica or nicotinic acid, each nutrient demonstrates neuro-protective and neuro-enhancing properties on their own.

For instance, in the case of nicotine (which becomes B-3 through oxidation), it has been known for some time that introduction of this substance improves the mental condition of dementia patients. In the journal *Psychopharmacology* 1992 (volume 108, pgs. 485-494), the authors of the study injected DAT (Dementia of Alzheimer's Type) patients with nicotine. It was found that, "these results demonstrate that DAT patients have significant perceptual and visual attentional deficits which are improved by nicotine administration." Keep in mind that this was with nicotine not nicotinic acid. But even with nicotinic acid or B-3 we should find the same results. Recent studies such as the one reported in *The Journal of Neuroscience*, 5 November 2008, which was titled 'Nicotinamide Restores Cognition in Alzheimer's Disease' have shown this. The subjects were mice that had Alzheimer's disease. When nicotinamide was administered to these mice the researchers found that the nutrient "restored cognitive deficits associated with pathology." The evidence was so convincing that the researchers concluded "that oral nicotinamide may represent a safe treatment for AD."

What is currently showing great promise for Alzheimer's patients is a natural substance known as curcumin. This compound is derived from the spice known as turmeric. Curcumin already had a long history of use in Indian medicine as a 'cleanser' before being discovered for its potential in neuro-diseases such as Alzheimer's. Modern medicine has re-discovered curcumin, so to speak, as a powerful anti-inflammatory. It has shown promise in preventing the growth of the plaques that are associated with Alzheimer's. The collective mind of the researchers, however, have missed an important fact concerning curcumin. This compound comes from turmeric and turmeric belongs to a specific family of plants known as Zingiberaceae. This family happens to be a silica accumulator. The phytolith content of the Zingiberaceae family is very high. Phytoliths are extremely small hydrated silica stones that are embedded in the epidermis of plants like tobacco. In other words, these plants are saturated with silica. Some plants like the Zingiberaceae have higher phytolith content than others. What is interesting is that curcumin, in studies, exhibits the same properties that silica would have. But this is because the active ingredient in curcumin is its *high silica content*.

SILICA IS MAGIC

The capacity of silica to balance pH, to prevent the fire in the brain, has to do with its incredible relationship and abilities with water. This is corroborated in nature and, amazingly, in recent findings in computer technology. Computer scientists have discovered a strange, almost fantastic sounding, property of silica just recently. It really should come as no surprise but they have found that silica *directs water flow* against gravity! The research was done at the University of Rochester and it was reported on the university website in March of 2010. "Researchers at the University of Rochester's Institute of Optics have discovered a way to make liquid flow vertically upward along a silicon surface, overcoming the pull of gravity, without pumps or other mechanical devices." The website goes on to say that silica can conduct water against the pull of gravity when the upright silica surface is physically altered by etching certain designs upon the surface of the silica with a high powered laser. The shape of the designs are not revealed in any article on the subject. "In a paper in the journal Optics Express, professor Chunlei Guo and his assistant Anatoliy Vorobyev demonstrate that by carving intricate patterns in silicon with extremely short, high-powered laser bursts, they can get liquid to climb to the top of a silicon chip like it was being sucked through a straw. Unlike a straw, though, there is no outside pressure pushing the liquid up; it rises on its own accord." Professor Chunlei Guo stated in an interview the implications of such a finding: "Imagine a huge waterway system shrunk down onto a tiny chip, like the electronic circuit printed on a microprocessor, so we can perform chemical or biological work with a tiny bit of liquid . . . blood could precisely travel along a certain path . . ."

This fascinating attraction or "suction" mechanism of silica is also seen in nature. How does water travel against gravity from the roots of plants to the leaves and upper regions of those plants? Keep in mind some plants such as the Redwood trees in California are 300 to 400 feet high. This is an astounding feat for water to be transported to the tallest regions of a Redwood. The dogma that is accepted in the botanical world is called Transpirational Pull or the Translocation of Sap. In this theory water is pulled up through the xylem by a sort of suction that is caused by the relative humidity of the surrounding atmosphere. It really gets even more complicated because there is another theory that goes along with the suction or 'pull' theory and that is the cohesion theory of hydrogen bonds which is all supposed to explain the upward movement of water in a plant.

But what is overlooked in all this is the composition of the xylem in plants. The xylem has been established as that part of the plant which serves as the main conduit for water flow. The xylem acts somewhat like the veins of the tree or plant conducting along the water and its contents otherwise known as sap. This much is not disputed. What is disputed is the method of water movement. How does it move upward? In the xylem of plants there are what is known as silica inclusions or silica grains. In some species such as the Laurel family of plants it has been established that there is a silica grain or inclusion for every cell of the secondary xylem. In light of the discovery that was noted above by the University of Rochester researchers we can see that the silica in plants is pulling or directing water against gravity just like in the experiments conducted by the researchers.

So we see that silica has the ability to direct water flow and as a result it is able to balance the acidity in a biological environment. Silica does this extremely efficiently by directing and/or attracting water to the important structures in the brain. Certain regions of the brain are composed of silica for a reason. Silica provides an oxygenated non-acidic environment for neurotransmitters to fire. When these regions become deficient in silica all sorts of neuro-pathologies begin to occur. Silica must constantly be supplied to the body through the diet but there is a problem with this as there is a lack of silica in the diet due to the refining of grains and sugar. This is nothing but the removal of the most important anti-inflammatory known to man.

WASTE MANAGER

Silica not only keeps the environment of the brain "clean" but it also keeps the human organism sanitary by removing waste. What is interesting in this connection is that everyone understands the role of fiber in keeping an individual's bowel movements 'regular'. But the actual fiber has nothing to do with bowel regularity— it is only acting as a carrier for silica. It is the rich silica composition of the fiber which draws water into the colon thereby expanding the fibrous material and increasing the water content and volume of the stools in the bowel making them softer and easier to pass. So here again we see the water directing/managing ability of silica. It is an overall management system for the entire organism by virtue of its affinity for water; whether it is in the brain or in the cells or in the colon, silica maintains the surrounding environment at optimal levels.

Oftentimes, when people decide to stop smoking, they will adopt a healthier diet which includes high fiber— hence, silica. This increased intake of silica is the actual reason for smoking cessation rather than 'willpower'. The simple reason for people smoking is that silica is removed from the food supply by food refining techniques. This mineral is not as prevalent in the diet as it should be. Whole grains are a big source of silica but the part that is the richest in silica, the hull and the bran, what we know as fiber, is stripped away in food processing. Rice is rich in silica but again it is in the hulls and bran — this is not the typical fare for most people as white rice is preferred. Even in the Far East, white rice is preferred over rice that has the bran and germ intact.

ENEMIES OF SILICA

The smoker makes a logical choice because of the benefits of silica in water/oxygen management. Again, in nature the element silicon is not found by itself. It is always bound to oxygen— we then call this combination silica or silicon di*oxide*. This mineral does the same thing in the brain, by attracting oxygen it creates an oxygen rich environment.

The enemy of silica is acid (or as we've come to know it, the FIRE) but not through direct action— silica itself is highly resistant to acidity but it needs to be replaced constantly because of what acidity does to the antagonist of silica and that is aluminum. Though aluminum is part of the brain structure, an imbalanced pH environment in the brain will release aluminum. Again, aluminum is an antagonist of silica. If there is a disproportion of aluminum to silica, aluminum may "push" silica out of system. This disproportion of aluminum to silica is always seen in cases of dementia and Alzheimer's.

This disproportion of aluminum due to over-acidity is seen in nature also. This happens to be the problem in ecosystems as when aluminum is released from soil due to acid rainfall and bullies other elements out of the system and displaces them— elements such as silicon. This aluminum makes its way into rivers and streams thereby polluting the wildlife. Because of this and other food processing techniques there seems to be a disproportion of aluminum in our environ-ment— it is even in most under-arm deodorants. Silica suffers an onslaught due to this contamination and due to the acidity caused by partial-foods consumption. The brain can not function efficiently without silica—much like a silicon chip in a computer is needed, so is the silicon in the brain.

The other enemy of silica is food fads. Health gurus and faddists have been pointing the finger of condemnation toward most grains as being the culprit behind ill-health and obesity. They are really throwing out the baby with the bathwater by not making simple distinctions. For example, sprouted grains and bread products are very healthy but they get lumped together with the zealous philosophy of "all grains are evil."

All these things make silica "unavailable" so to speak. When this happens it's not long before the body will reorient itself to acquire silica in a non-food substance, whatever it may be.

But this urge for the nonfood substance will cease once silica is supplied in the diet through supplements and/or food.

CHAPTER 6: THE END OF STARVATION IS THE END OF SMOKING

The true value of any theory lies in its utility— that is, does it work? If everything that has been said up to this point is true about *why* you smoke, then the application of this truth will be successful. If we know the "why" of smoking we should be able to answer the "how" of quitting. The *how* is precisely what this chapter is all about.

Applying the following principles will lead you to a place you haven't experienced since before you began smoking. The place where cigarette cravings are nonexistent. The place where you never have to worry about them coming back either.

To get to that place you have to follow the map— this chapter. But you may have noticed that destinations on maps have a few ways of getting to them and that choosing a specific road is largely a choice left up to the individual. Not everyone likes main roads. Some people like taking back roads to avoid traffic. The destination, becoming completely craving-free, is yours and easily achieved— as long as silica and vitamin B3 are your "mode of transportation", so to speak. But there are different forms of silica and various ways to incorporate it into your diet. The different 'roads' to the final destination are the unique preferences and tastes that each person has. So, carefully consider the options and approaches in the coming pages and see which 'road' grabs you, fits in and works well with your lifestyle.

THERE'S NO TRYING IN QUITTING

A few words of clarification before we begin. When you start to add silica rich foods and/or supplements to your diet, there is one thing you need to understand: Do not, in any way, *try* to quit smoking while adding silica to your diet.

Really.

You must continue to smoke as you normally do. This method doesn't require you to be "strong" or any such thing remotely pertaining to the invocation of willpower. Many people feel, at the outset, that they need to "help the process along", so to speak, by doing this. There is absolutely no willpower involved in this. What you'll be doing by adding silica to your diet is feeding a starving body and mind. When this is done successfully, the cravings for the alternate form of silica (cigarettes) will go away.

Think of it in this way. If you're hungry you know what to do. You go to the fridge and look for something or hop into a car and go to a restaurant or grocery store. The goal of this is to put food in your mouth and into your stomach so you can feel full. Once you start eating food you surely do not need willpower to convince yourself that soon you'll be feeling full. That would be absurd. The hunger takes care of itself because you are feeding it. No willpower involved.

In the same way, silica in the right amount from a good food and/or supplement source will take care of the desire to smoke. The desire to quit will come naturally. There's no need to be anxious or to worry at all. What you'll discover will pleasantly surprise you.

THREE GENERAL PRINCIPLES

There are THREE preliminary principles that you need to know about before we get to the directions. These are the guiding principles that must govern your use of silica. Bear them always in mind. These principles DO NOT apply to vitamin B3 so much as they do to silica. The reason is because silica is far more important in smoking cessation. In essence, all three principles are really just common-sense applied. Read through them for now but remember to come back and make sure you fully grasp them— they're that important.

So here goes. In the first few days to one week you will need to take silica with

1) Regularity

2) in the Right amounts

3) in the Right form.

The extent to which you apply these principles correctly is the extent to which how quickly you'll be able to quit smoking. IF applied correctly, smoking cessation occurs within 24 hours to three days. Sometimes in just hours. At the most, no longer than 7 days. Again, it depends on how close these principles are adhered to.

1) Regularity

Think of the way you smoke. You do it with *regularity*. Every hour or two, or whatever interval it is, you get the itch and then you smoke. If you are going to quit with any celerity you must do the same with this nutrient— at least in the beginning.

This principle must become ingrained within you. If you take silica once a day and report that it isn't working for you then you're not paying attention. For some reason, even when this principle is explicitly stated, it seems to go over some people's heads. Don't be that person.

The point is that in the first few days you will have to be zealous, in a sense, about your intake of silica— you must be mindful of the clock or your own internal sense.

Not only will you be amazed at the results but you will find that, once you go through this initial phase of diligent intake of silica, you won't need as much silica as you did at that initial phase. Many people have reported that they need less than half the regular intake as when they first started and some even less.

The important thing is that you have to build up (build down?) to that point. That's why the inital phase is important. In the beginning stages your body will be "hungry" for silica and will horde it. You need to supply it regularly to send the body a message that it will keep receiving silica.

How can you tell if you're taking it with the correct regularity? You will have no cravings for cigarettes. Simple as that.

So a good rule of thumb to follow would be: *If you are craving cigarettes that means you need more silica either in frequency (regularity) or amount— or you need to change the form.*

2) Right Amounts

What if you took a shower with only a few drops of water? Obviously you have enough sensibility to know how much you need when it comes to this. You need the *right amount* of water to clean the body for your size and weight and however much dirt is on you. There are factors involved that you naturally take account of when showering. Unfortunately this same sensibility is lost in most people who supplement. When you use silica you need the right amount for your situation in order for it to work because there are many variables involved with your specific body type and the degree to which you are bereft of this nutrient. You intuitively know how much more water you need to rinse off the dirt in a shower. This analogy can also pertain to the principle of frequency.

So think about this for a second. Can someone else tell you how much water you need for that shower and at what frequency? Hardly. You're the best judge of that. Anyone else might be able to give you a *guideline* or tell you what worked for them but in the end you are the only one who can only determine that.

Do you get it? In the following pages I'm going to give you guidelines and general ideas about how much and how frequently but in the end only you can determine correctly. A teaspoon of this or that works for some but others may need a tablespoon and instead of three times a day their optimum frequency might be five times a day. *Do you get it?*

Think about that shower when you supplement with silica.

3) Right Form

This is the most important principle. If the silica you're taking is not able to be absorbed then it won't matter how much or how frequent you take silica.

You need to take the *right form* of silica—in other words, this principle boils down to . . . your ability to absorb minerals. Digestion. The fact is, silica comes in many forms and some forms may not be as easily digested. If you have good digestion any silica product will work. Not so much if your digestion is poor.

And a growing number of people are not digesting as they should be for whatever reasons.

If you find that you fall into this category of inadequate digestion— there is no need to worry. There are forms of silica that can overcome even the worst of compromised digestive systems.

I recommend taking the most absorbable form of silica. But if you feel you have decent digestion, any silica supplement will work. (see next heading for ratings). Also, taking probiotics through certain foods like yogurt and sauerkraut (unpasteurized) or even supplements will help you with your digestion. Once you go on a program of increased probiotic intake for a while, you'll then be able to digest **any** silica supplement. I can't emphasize enough how important this is for many of the readers. If you do even a superficial research of the matter, you'll find studies have shown that improved gut health solves many conditions of ill-health. Now, the underlying reason for this may escape some but what it really comes down to is that **increasing healthy bacteria will improve mineral absorption.** This is the real reason why health is improved. A good probiotic is available from Garden of Life called Primal Defense. There are others. Do some research. I think the best approach is fermented foods but a supplement can definitely help and could be a good combinatory approach if you also eat fermented foods. If you're serious about this you won't have to worry about which silica supplement works for you because all of them will— even the ones considered cheaper and therefore less absorbable. This is all up to you. If you've had antibiotics more than once or many times, and if you're a sugar-holic then I would definitely recommend doing this first (replenishing good bacteria) and persevere with it. You can start really cheap by eating yogurt or other fermented foods, and then build your way up to a good probiotic supplement. When good gut bacteria increases then the amounts and frequency of the silica supplement that you need to stop smoking won't be as much. Most people ignore this advice and do well anyway. That may be you. In the end it will be up to you to decide where you stand. If you find you need inordinate amounts of the best silica supplement then you need help with your gut health.

To sum up: if you are taking the silica supplement **regularly** and in the **right amounts** and you have sub-par results, then you need to either change the silica product to the most digestible form or take an intensive course of probiotics and then any silica product will work.

SILICA SUPPLEMENTS RATED

Here are the most used silica supplements rated as to their absorption, hence effectiveness: (If any of these is no longer being produced please contact me)

1. **Orgono Living Silica-Collagen Booster** liquid (22.5 mg per serving) This silica is in the form of monomethylsilanetriol. It is the most absorbable silica and so, the best that I know of at this time. It will work on just about anyone, even with people that have the most compromised digestion. The company that makes this product (Silicium Laboratories) has a few other products that are somewhat confusingly also called Living Silica. So, to make sure you have the right one, make sure it is the one that has 22.5 mg per serving— and the label on the bottle will say *Collagen Booster*. Do NOT get the product called Sports Recovery silica or the one called Siliplant or the one that only has 12 mg per serving. More silica per serving is better and they are all around the same price anyway.

I will share case histories concerning this product but let's get through the other silica products first.

2. **Orgono Silica Powder**

This particular silica is also made by Silicium Laboratories with the exception that it is in powder form. Most people are able to digest this and have great success with it.

3. **Eidon Ionic Silica** 18 oz. (liquid) The Eidon company is one of a few that make ionic silica. Ionic silicas are all pretty much the same as far as digestibility and effectiveness. However, even with the ionic form there is a minority that can't fully digest it. It's a good form of silica and I have used it with great effectiveness but it just doesn't work with every single person. If you feel you have decent digestion and this form is readily available to you then I would try it.

4. **Oceanic Silica** (capsules–Solgar) Through the years I have personally relied on this product. However, for some, it is not as easily absorbed as the top three. I would give it about a 70% effectiveness rating. In other words, it acts effectively in about 7 out of ten people.

5. **Bamboo silica** (capsules–various brands) About the same ef-

fectiveness as the Oceanic Silica.

There are many other brands and varieties. These five are the ones that were most used by, and available to, individuals around the globe.

Important: DO NOT TAKE SILICA THAT IS DERIVED FROM HORSETAIL HERB OR HAS HORSETAIL IN IT. The horsetail herb (not the silica) may have side effects if taken long term. There are some silica supplements, not many, that contain the horsetail herb. One of them is called FloraSil. It has horsetail in it. **Do not get it.** Not that it's harmful due to the silica but more rather that long term use isn't recommended because of the horsetail component in it. Also, be aware that some companies market their silica supplement as a 'complex'; which means that the silica in the capsule will be bound with other ingredients, most likely horsetail herb. Long story short: Check the ingredients of your silica supplement to make sure that it does not contain horsetail. Of course, the five products mentioned above do not contain horsetail.

Once again, if you're digestion is decent then any of these supplements will work. If it's not you can always improve it by focusing on taking probiotics— then any supplement will work.

WHAT ABOUT B3?

Hardly anyone has an issue with vitamin B3 absorption. Average digestion or bad digestion— doesn't matter when it comes to B3. The only thing concerning B3 is that there are so many different brands yet broadly speaking there are two general categories: Food based and chemically derived types of B3. If possible try to obtain a food based B3 rather than the chemical forms. Garden of Life has a food based B Complex and a multivitamin line that contains B3. I've had great results with both chemically-derived B3 in the form of niacin and niacinamide and also with the food based B3 vitamins. If you do get niacin (chemically derived) then make sure you get the flush-free niacin. I realize that the flush does have some benefits and I confess I loved the experience of the so-called "flush" but I've found that some aren't too keen on this effect— so I tend to recommend the no-flush niacin. It works just as well as regular niacin for smoking cessation.

The frequency and amounts with which you take vitamin B3 will be much less than with silica. In smoking cessation silica is the nutrient that is primary— it is more important than B3 and thus must be emphasized to a greater extent in your intake. Taking vitamin B3 just three times daily should suffice for most people if you're taking niacin or niacinamide. If you're taking a food based B3 just two times a day should be good enough. Another thing to keep in mind is that B3 belongs to a family known as the B complex group. They work well together so consider down the road getting a B complex vitamin.

IN THE LION'S DEN

What will happen to you when you take silica in the **right amount**, in the **right form**, and with **regularity**?

Here's an example that occurred in 2011 to a young man named Jon who had smoked close to 20 cigarettes a day (one American pack) for just over 10 years.

I'm going to relate Jon's story in bullet-point form:

-Jon downloads the ebook (**You Are Not Addicted To Cigarette Smoking You Are Starving** was in ebook form in 2011) on a Friday

-Jon reads book Friday night and into Saturday.

-When Jon gets through with the "magic" chapter (his words in describing the chapter which gives the specific directions) he promptly runs to the healthfood store to get silica (He already had niacin at home).

-Jon starts his silica routine on Sunday morning.

-Sunday night Jon notices a distinct "off" flavor to each cigarette.

-On Monday Jon can barely smoke half a pack of cigarettes (10 cigarettes)

-On Tuesday Jon follows the same silica regimen but he is now down to 5 cigarettes a day. However, each time he smokes a cigarette he is only smoking half a cigarette. So, in reality it's something less than five cigarettes.

-On Wednesday John finds that he has absolutely NO desire to smoke. At all.

-On Thursday . . . Well, this is where it gets interesting.

Jon continues his silica routine. But this is Thursday and that means poker night for Jon and several of his friends— who happen to smoke cigarettes and cigars profusely at these gatherings. Nevertheless, Jon fearlessly trods into the usual smoke-filled room to play with his comrades . . . but then proceeds to trudge out of the gathering about 30 minutes later.

Jon called it an early night not because he was losing at the game, nor was it because he was being tempted to smoke by the incessant smoking of his cohorts. He left for only one reason: The cigarette and cigar smoke that permeated the room was utterly *repugnant* to him. Five days into his silica routine and Jon fully realized he could not stand the smell of cigarettes . . . or cigars for that matter. But not only that— even the idea, the very thought of smoking, was abhorrent to him. So he walked out.

In fact, he became so sensitive to tobacco smoke that he could smell it on people's clothes as they walked by him on sidewalks. In short, within a week's time he became one of the worst people you'd want to meet if you were a smoker!

Now, I want you to grasp something. Normally when someone begins a smoking cessation program there is some trepidation about one thing— being tempted to smoke. Everyone trying to quit has a healthy fear of situations, thoughts, or even people that might trigger the urge to smoke.

Jon's behavior was the exact opposite of being tempted.

But this is what happens when you incorporate silica into your diet. As Jon found, not only will your desires vanish, you will be absolutely impervious to any temptation to smoke.

So you must be wondering . . .

WHAT DID JON DO?

When Jon went to the store that night, seven years ago, he bought the silica product that was available. He grabbed the last two 18 oz. bottles of a product called Eidon Silica Supplement. (Number 3 on the list above)

Now, Jon had an idea, a guideline, of how much to take from my ebook. But Jon intuitively felt that he needed more than the usual amount for his silica intake. He is six feet tall, just slightly over 200 hundred pounds and a male. These things matter— not to mention many of the other variables involved such as absorption ability. Remember the shower analogy?

So he took certain things into account and being mindful of these things decided on the following plan:

The first 2 days, Jon took the supplement 6 times a day two tablespoons each time about 2 to three hours apart. Notice something: he was definitely diligent in observing the *principle of regularity* mentioned above. On two of the occasions that he took silica, he added one niacin tablet 300mg (no flush). So, the niacin was just twice a day for those two days. Remember, silica is more important— you simply will not need as much niacin as you will silica.

Now, for Jon, the workweek was approaching and he didn't wan't to be burdened with the 6 times a day routine so he took the supplement 3 times a day four tablespoons each time for the next 4 days. Each time on an empty stomach. Once in the morning after awaking, once before lunch and once before dinner.

Pay attention to his reasoning again. Since he would be taking the supplement less periodically (with less regularity) than the first two days, he reasoned that he would have to at least increase the amounts for those 3 times a day— so he began taking 4 tablespoons 3 times a day. Yes, this is a significant increase but Jon saw the remarkable results of those two days and he decided he was going full steam ahead. Would I have recommended that amount? Probably not because I'm not sure that that amount can be absorbed in the first place. But it worked for him.

Also, what is important to mention is that Jon at no time *tried* to quit. I'm bringing this up again because the only thing you should be focusing on is your silica intake. Do not make this painful for yourself. If you're diligent with your silica intake you'll see the drop off in desire immediately. So I encourage you to keep smoking as you normally would. Just concentrate on your silica intake and you will be pleasantly surprised.

After surveying this approach of Jon's, one thing should stand out: Jon was on a warpath.

To put it in other words, Jon knew from his reading of the ebook that silica demand is constant— especially for someone who is starving for it. And that's what a smoker is: An individual who is starving for a specific nutrient. In the beginning stages this need must be attended to with a zealous regularity.

Jon told me repeatedly in the ensuing years that it was the easiest thing he had ever done. The only thing he had to do was focus on his silica intake, especially during the initial period.

Now, Jon quit smoking after 3 days. However, he kept that routine of 4 tablespoons 3 times a day for about two weeks.

Jon felt, after about two weeks of doing that routine, that he did not need to have the same amount of silica. He lessened the total amount he needed per day but he increased the regularity.

Pay attention now. Here is what he did:

Instead of taking doses at certain intervals during the day Jon decided to have silica all day!

What does that even mean? Before Jon read my book and began silica he had the habit of drinking about 6 to 7 water bottles a day (16 oz). So, after his silica **saturation** stage, he decided to use this habit of water drinking to his advantage for his **maintenance** phase. By putting ONE tablespoon of the Eidon Silica into each bottle he could sip these "silica water bottles" throughout the day— a regular dose of silica throughout the day in his drinking water. He drank water regularly anyway— so why not add some silica?

It was pretty ingenious because every few minutes or so he was getting a regular dose of silica. Certain days and certain bottles he would put two tablespoons in. This was based on perceived stress levels he knew he would be facing in the future of that particular day. In his case, busy periods at his restaurant. Even though that one tablespoon is a low dose he made up for it by the regularity with which he was taking it. Also, he had fed his body adequately in the initial **saturation phase** which is the first few days to a week.

In those first two weeks he had saturated and quenched the body's need for silica. Because of this there was a drop in his need for silica. This drop-off happens with everyone who is persistent with silica intake at the beginning. If you're conscientious at the beginning you won't need as much silica later. What that point of transition is I couldn't tell you because it varies with everyone. With some it's three days. Others take about one to two weeks like Jon. Still others need more time like a month before they need less levels. One thing is for sure, it happens.

As I hope you've noticed there's a difference in the two phases—*saturation phase* and *maintenance phase*. For example, if Jon used his maintenance approach at the beginning stage (the saturation phase) he may not have been as successful. It would have taken him much longer to quit.

To sum up: After about two weeks Jon entered the *maintenance phase*. The initial stage (the *saturation phase*) is where you must feed the desperate hunger that your body is having for the silica mineral. The different phases call for different requirements of silica. *Some people can not or will not, for whatever reason, get this distinction.* I don't know why this happens but it's been my experience.

What ends up happening is they take maintenance amounts during the time when their body is *screaming* for saturation amounts. If you get the distinction between the two phases you won't have any problems.

Nevertheless, I feel that we must put a picture to this. If you go without eating a morsel of food for three or four days, how hungry do you think you'll feel? Picture it, feel it. Now picture going to a restaurant after that period of hunger. You will eat well. You won't gorge to make yourself sick . . . but you will eat well. And you will probably eat more than usual, at least that first day or so. Right?

Let's stay with this picture. You are starving after four days of no food. For the sake of argument, suppose that there arises a complicating factor, another fictitious scenario: No matter what restaurant you go to to quell your hunger pains, you are told that all you can have is a small portion of an appetizer. That's it. And no matter where you go in this make-believe setting, all you are offered is little morsels of food. Of course, your appetite is raging for two burgers with large fries and this fanciful realm stops you from getting what you need. Here you can only have a few fries. How would you like to go to a pizza place in this condition and have them tell you that you can only have one slice of pizza?

Cruel isn't it? How would you feel?

Let's keep going. What if I came along after a few days of this treatment you're receiving from everyone and asked you "Hey, have you gotten over your hunger?" You would bite my head off. The reason is that after that starvation period of four days you still are not having enough food in the right regularity and in the right amounts.

You're starving and these dribs and drabs of food are not doing the job of quelling your hunger. All you want to do is get out of that desperate hunger stage so you can go back to your normal routine. Your normal maintenance routine. Get it?

This is what you must grasp from this fictitious scenario— the fact that you can't get over your long-standing hunger by barely feeding your self. The same principle applies to silica intake because it is a specific hunger. To repeat: If you give your body just dribs and drabs of silica, *for which it has been starving for a long time*, you will never get over your hunger. Therefore, you must feed your body well in the beginning stages with silica . . . in the right amounts and with regularity and in an absorbable form. Because your body is starving.

MONEY

So, now let's get to an aspect of this method that hits close to home . . . the pocketbook. When Jon went into *maintenance mode* it cost him about $18.00 a week because the bottle at that dosage lasted one week. The first two weeks–the *saturation stage*–cost him $36.00 per week which was two bottles per week. In 2019 that price is about $40.00 per week for two bottles for the *saturation phase* and $20.00 per week for one bottle of the Eidon Silica for the *maintenance phase*.

Amazing when you consider that he was spending $84.00 a week in cigarettes. What's $40 per week for two weeks if it stops your habit dead in its tracks for good? And what's $18.00 a week to maintain that? In the big scheme of things, it's nothing.

However, Jon was something of an extreme case. Many have found that it costs even less in the maintenance phase. A bottle may last two weeks or more especially if you incorporate foods rich in silica, as we'll see.

The idea to keep in mind in all of this is that silica is important in health anyway (see previous chapter). This is a mineral that is vital, though it is not publicized as such. It is not only keeping you off cigarettes it is doing much more.

Let's get back to Jon. What is going on today with him? He still likes the Eidon Silica supplement but he uses even less than when he was in his maintenance phase. He only uses two or three bottles of water per day with one tablespoon of silica. The reason for this? He incorporates more silica-rich foods into his diet. We'll get into this approach more in the following pages.

Not everyone ends up combining. Most people prefer to continue taking strictly supplements even years later. That is perfectly fine because supplements are convenient and the amounts needed, after a certain period of time, decrease anyway.

Overall the Eidon supplement was a success for Jon. He had good absorption, obviously, because his desires waned immediately and then ceased completely within 3 days.

Jon's intake for ionic silica was the upper limit of what people that used ionic silica took.

In other words, if you're not getting results from the upper limit of intake that Jon established then you need to switch to a more aborbable silica.

WHAT SHOULD YOU DO?

The serving size of Eidon Silica is one tablespoon per serving.

Eidon carries two sizes/concentrations of silica. These instructions are for the 18 ounce bottle which Jon used— not the concentrated form which is only a few ounces (If you get the concentrated form or if that's all that's available for you contact me)

Take one tablespoon 3 times daily in just a few ounces of water. Preferably on an empty stomach. When you first awake. Before lunch. And once before dinner. Those are your three periodic times.

In addition to this, put one to two tablespoons of Eidon into a water bottle to sip throughout the day. This is your sipping bottle. Do this for your first two to three bottles. Hopefully you drink at least three water bottles a day.

Also take vitamin B3 in some form. Garden of Life Vitamin Code multivitamin is a good one to take. Two capsules daily. Or you can buy niacin in a wide range of doses. One 250mg (or even 300mg) tablet or capsule twice a day should be enough. You can get lower doses like 100mg which I feel are even better because you can get a steady supply of b3 throughout the day by taking 2 or 3 tablets/capsules.

There are other ionic silica supplements like the brand *Good State Liquid Ionic Silica*. If you get this one do the same thing. The only difference would be the serving size. Good State's serving size is one teaspoon. So all you need to do is use the same method as Eidon but just plug in the teaspoon size for the daily requirements. For example, instead of one tablespoon per water bottle use one teaspoon and so on. This goes for any other ionic silica that's out there. Use their recommended serving size and then follow the protocol I just gave.

This is the baseline for this product. Most people got excellent results with this approach. But it will vary person to person— you may need more in terms of quantity per serving or you may need to increase the frequency with which you take it. It depends on the results you're getting. If you get excellent results that very first day— keep going. Maybe put two tablespoons of Eidon into the sipping bottles on day two? Or take it four times a day instead of three? Remember, you're starving for a particular mineral. Regularity. Right amounts.

Here's the sign that you should be looking for— on the second day of this you should be smoking much less than normal. If you're not disgusted with smoking by the third day you may need to switch the silica supplement to a more absorbable form.

Again, in my experience this supplement will work for most but there is a small percentage who have difficulty absorbing it.

Thankfully, there is a supplement with even better absorption that we will look at now.

WHAT DID ZACH DO?

Zach would readily admit to you that he could be a poster child for silica products. There hardly is one that he hasn't tried. The reason for this was poor absorption. The variety of silica products that he used worked— to a certain extent. For example, from his usual 20 cigarettes a day he was down to 4 or 5 a day while using the Eidon Ionic Silica that Jon used. This was a significant drop but it still was frustrating, in a sense, because Zach and I both felt that if a more absorbable silica product was out there, he wouldn't even desire those 4 or 5 cigarettes.

Zach kept the faith and eventually discovered the product that finally did it for him: **Orgono Organic Silica Powder–** by a company called Silicium Laboratories.

Here is the routine he followed:

One rounded teaspoon per 20 oz. of water four times daily. But he administered it in a special way as we'll soon see. (There is a small scoop that comes with the container. About three of these scoops equals a rounded teaspoon. You can discard the scoop and just use a teaspoon measure if you want)

By the way, "rounded" means that it is not as precise as, say, a level teaspoon. In a rounded teaspoon you will have a little 'mound' or 'hill' above the scoop. So, in a sense, it's a bit more than a precise level teaspoon.

Let's get to how Zach became completely and totally smoke free, shedding those last four or five cigs, within three days. Remember the technique that Jon used above in his *maintenance phase*? Jon drank water throughout the day with ionic silica in it. This is exactly what Zach did except he did this during the *saturation phase*. This was a most genious innovation by Zach that he felt was dictated by need and circumstance.

Obviously, what's helpful is that Zach, like Jon, are both consistent water drinkers.

Zach used his 20 oz. water bottle that he would drink from and refill throughout the day. He added one rounded teaspoon of the Orgono powder to the 20 ounces of water. (The powder dissolves by itself within a few minutes. No need to shake.) Zach would then drink from this until it was gone. He then refiled and added another teaspoon to his water bottle three more times during that day. Sometimes sipping, sometimes guzzling, Zach made his way through about 80 ounces of "silica water" each day and by the fourth day he was completely smoke-free and has been since (three years as of this writing).

Freedom in four days. No more lingering four or five cigarettes for Zach. He found the silica that worked for him. Zach dubbed this method the *"drip-feed"* method— much like an iv bag used in hospitals, there is a steady flow or "drip" making its way into the human body via your water bottle. In the same way Zach, whenever he sipped water, was getting a steady inflow of silica . . . all day, throughout the day.

His intake of vitamin B3 was from a multivitamin by Garden of Life. He only had one capsule per day of this multivitamin and it surprisingly seemed to cover his need for B3. Silica is primary.

Why did Zach need the drip-feed method? Zach felt that periodically dosing every couple hours or so wouldn't work for him. He felt that he needed silica all day long with every sip of water he took—and this worked. Remember Jon's case? Jon did this approach in his "maintenance phase". Again, the only difference here is that Zach used this technique for his "saturation phase" which is the first phase. He made sure that he had enough silica though in this initial stage. So, the drip-feed technique can be used in either stage as long as you're wary of your needs.

Can you take it every couple hours, or so, as a periodic dose without doing the "drip feed" method? Absolutely. There are people that have done that successfully with this particular product. If you do that you'll want to take it, as best you can, on an empty stomach. You'll use less water of course (or juice). What would the dose be for this particular supplement? It would be the same (one rounded teaspoon four times a day in a little bit of water or juice) except that you'd be taking the dose in one sitting and then waiting a few hours before the next one.

The only problem I see with periodic dosing is that sometimes people forget to take their dose of silica or they take it at a longer interval which really doesn't put the kibosh on the desires. As I've stated before, you really need, in the first day or so, to keep on top of your silica intake. If you are lax in this attention then what's the sense of even doing it? Saturation in the first day or so is the only way to quell the desires. Remember: When you feel a desire to smoke you probably need more silica or you don't have the right product.

Now here is something remarkable, yet expected: Zach doesn't take the same amount as he once did. Of course, this is expected because your body doesn't need as much silica after you feed it properly at first. The difference with Zach is how little he needs now. Sometimes he goes a few days without taking silica. Not recommended but I'm reporting what he has told me.

I believe that what enables Zach to do this is how assiduous he was with incorporating silica into his daily life at the beginning. In other words, he fed his body well, with silica, and his body gave him back a message saying it didn't need as much silica. This change occurred in several months time.

Zach still uses the same product. These days he can gauge how much silica he needs. He just seems to "know". Usually it's one teaspoon per day in a bottle of water. Obviously, there's not a chance that he could have used these amounts in the beginning stages— he never would have quit with that dosage.

Here's the skipping record again: I can't stress enough how, in the beginning, you really have to be on top of your silica intake. Don't get off guard and be presumptuous. There are going to be times when you feel you don't need silica at all because the desire is so far away from you and you'll even begin wondering whether the fact that you smoking for 20 years was really just a psychological issue. Silica can put you in that place of absolute confidence because the process is so easy. I too have experienced the feeling of: "Hey wait a minute. Maybe the silica is just a placebo. This is just too easy. Maybe this whole thing was just a psychological thing and silica isn't really needed. I can do without it."

Quite a few people have stumbled because of this. Again, it's because the process is so incredibly easy. In one to three days your cravings have completely vanished. They are nowhere in sight. Then pride steps in. "I accomplished this thing on my own, right?" Willpower alone? And so you neglect to take silica. A few days becomes a week, maybe more, and then it happens— you smell or see a cigarette and something is triggered inside you. The old cravings comes back, bigger and stronger than before.

Do not fall into that trap.

If you find yourself in this situation just get back up, dust your clothes off and get back on the silica wagon. Remember, we need silica. Make it a part of your life. In the beginning stages you must successfully build a reserve of the mineral and let your body adapt to the new levels— the amount of time varies depending on the person. The part that doesn't take much time is the cessation of smoking. The more diligent you are in your intake the faster the desires will leave.

Let's get back to this product. The only concern that people might have with this supplement is that there are approximately 2 to 3 grams of maltodextrin per serving. So if you're taking it in the same amounts as Zach did then you're taking in about 12 grams of sugar a day. There is no need for alarm at this. Let's do some comparisons. How about those sports drinks that people take? You're talking about 30 to 60 grams per serving. Yes, per serving. What about that cup of coffee with 2 or 3 spoons of sugar or those donuts or how about that soda or two you had with that pizza. Compare that to 12 grams per day from a product that enables you to stop smoking with ease and quickness.

I'd say that's a great deal. Especially if you consider that inevitably the dosage will go down.

WHAT SHOULD YOU DO?

I'd say follow Zach's protocol to the tee. One heaping teaspoon dissolved in a bottle of water (16 ounces or slightly more like Zach) four times daily. You don't have to shake it to mix in, just let it sit for a minute or three.

If you're not a big water drinker you can take it periodically, say, three times a day at first, one teaspoon in just a little bit of water or juice (a few ounces or so). However, it would also be a good idea to at least have one sipping bottle around during the day to occassionally drink from. If you can do two, that's even better.

This product works pretty much with everyone. But there are some cases where absorption is so poor that an even more absorptive product is called for. Also, diabetics might be wary of the sugar content (even though I feel it's low) of the Orgono powder. Happily, there is a supplement that answers these needs and more.

WHAT DID JENNA DO?

I'm going to introduce a couple of individuals who, in my experience, had the least ability to absorb silica. In one of the cases there was also the complicating factor of diabetes. But the product they used (**Living Silica-Collagen Booster**) helped them overcome their extreme malabsorption for silica like no other product.

Jenna had type 2 diabetes and smoked incessantly (20 to 25 cigarettes a day). Not one of the silica products worked for her except for the Orgono Silica powder but she became worried when she realized the sugar content.

The most absorbable form of silica is monomethylsilanetriol. Yes, it's a mouthful but this form of silica works . . . every time.

The same company that makes the Orgono silica powder also makes this product. The company actually has two products with this form of silica. They are both called **Living Silica** liquid. The one you want has the subtitle of **Collagen Booster**. So it should say **Liquid Silica-Collagen Booster** on the bottle. BE SURE TO GET THE ONE THAT HAS 22.5 mg PER SERVING. Also, it comes in different bottle sizes— 500mg or 1000mg. The larger size is a much better deal.

Day one: Jenna took it 8 times that very first day (about two hours apart). One tablespoon with a few ounces of water each time. She could only smoke 12 cigarettes that day. Compared to what she normally smoked this was a great improvement.

Day two: She felt she was on the right track because her desires were curtailed the day before. So she decided to take it 10 times on this day— one tablespoon each time with a bit of water. Total cigarettes smoked? Five.

Day three: Same dosage and times per day as day two. On this day she could hardly bear the thought of smoking— she only smoked three cigarettes . . . with difficulty.

Day Four: Same dosage as days two and three. She had no desire to smoke whatsoever.

During this whole time she also took one capsule of niacin (non-flush) three times per day. The capsules contained 300mg of niacin each.

Not only did she stop smoking with ease but she felt, as she said, "lighter, more clear" in her thoughts and in her attitude. Many people have experienced this very same thing. The freedom that you feel from breaking the chains of the dreadful habit is almost intoxicating.

Can you put a price on that?

Actually you can. Quitting smoking and the attendant freedom, that lightness of being that Jenna experienced? $49.95 1st week for the one bottle of Living Silica by Orgono (1000mg) Once again there are two sizes– 1000mg and 500mg. I would get the larger one because it ends up being cheaper.

After that first week Jenna continued to take the product five to six times a day for two months. One tablespoon each time. This came to about $25.00 a week because the 1000mg bottle lasted two weeks.

After that 2 month period she felt she only needed it three times a day. One bottle of the Living Silica now lasted three weeks on this regimen of three tablespoons per day. One tablespoon three times daily. This comes to just over $15.00 a week. Three times daily is the routine that she follows to this day eighteen months later.

As you can see, the same thing happened to her as with everyone else that does this correctly in the initial stages— the need for silica, inevitably, diminishes.

A stark example of this is a gentleman by the name of Henry who took the **Living Silica** 10 times daily— with the first few doses being a double dose! What stands out about Henry's approach is that it had him quitting smoking by the end of that very first day. Henry did what he called the "ratio method". In other words, he matched each cigarette he smoked to a dose of silica. One to one ratio. Just the first ten cigarettes though. Anything more than that probably means you have an absorption issue and you need to fix it with a course of probiotics.

Henry normally smoked a pack a day (20 cigarettes). He decided to take a dose of the **Living Silica** right before smoking a cigarette. He was determined to do this for his **first ten cigarettes of the day**. What Henry found is that by the sixth cigarette the taste was so off-putting that he could barely go on. He ended up just taking a few puffs of his last four cigarettes. He barely made it to ten cigarettes. He could not go on with the rest of the pack. He was done smoking for that day and, amazingly, forever. This from a man who had smoked a pack a day for 30 years.

In the first few days he took vitamin B3 in the form of niacinamide 250mg per capsule. He took one capsule three times a day.

If you were to follow this regimen this is what you would do. Henry's first three cigarettes were paired to a double dose of the **Liv-**

ing Silica (2 tablespoons) with a little water. So, take two tablespoons with a little water and then smoke your cigarette. Cigarettes four through ten were paired with one tablespoon of the **Living Silica** in a little bit of water. So, take one tablespoon with a little water and then smoke your cigarette . . . if you can.

On the second day he took it eight times— every one to two hours. He continued this routine for about a week. After that first week, he started taking it 4 times a day two tablespoons each time. He did this for about a month and then he got into ultra-maintenance mode and to this day (two years later), he takes the same product 2 to 4 times a day as a double dose. That is quite a contrast as you can see compared to that very first day.

Why am I bringing up extreme cases? To demonstrate that some people are more starving, more deficient in this mineral than others—one size does not fit all. You may need more than the average person as these two did. There are factors involved that require some people to take more for the silica to have an effect. Henry did consider his age, his weight, and the fact that he was male (men seem to need more). But these are objective factors and Henry didn't totally go by just these facts. What Henry and Jenna did do was gauge their desires. They didn't start out thinking they were going to take it 8 times a day or 10 times a day. What they did was say to themselves: **If I feel the desire to smoke that means I am not taking enough silica in frequency or in amount.**

In other words, if you feel this particular product is working—say the cigarette tastes funny or you notice you didn't finish your last cigarette, etc, etc—then you're going in the right direction. Don't back off. Put the pedal to the metal and start taking more incrementally . . . within reason.

Here's an anecdote, that I think about often, to demonstrate how you must think about this: Not too long ago a certain individual had been taking silica and was successful . . . to a point. She previously smoked around 10 to 12 cigarettes a day. Her silica intake brought her down to 2 to 3 cigarettes a day. She was rather happy but yet perplexed that she couldn't seem to "shake" those 2 or 3 cigarettes a day. This had been going on for about two weeks when she contacted me. She told me the situation and I gave her the simple answer: "Take more silica."

"Take more silica? But you told me to take it three times a day."

"Yes. But that was just a baseline." That was the part that she didn't hear originally. What I gave her was a general guide and that she would have to determine her needs ultimately. She did increase the frequency (not the amount) with which she took silica and the lingering desire for those two or three cigarettes faded away completely.

Regularity. Right amounts. Right product. Whenever the slightest inkling of a desire to smoke "pops up", that means you're not doing one of those three things correctly.

Hopefully, you'll be taking silica in the right amounts and regularity of intake so you won't have to confront cravings just "popping up" out of nowhere. If you take the preemptive stance, that your silica intake will be at the forefront of your daily routine, then no cravings will occur at all.

WHAT SHOULD YOU DO?

I quite like the ratio method for the **Living Silica-Collagen Booster** product but I would also prepare a "sipping bottle" (as in the example from Zach) in conjunction with the ratio method. This will fill in the gaps between your silica doses. The sipping bottle could be one or two tablespoons per bottle. I would make about two to three of these a day if you're doing the ratio method. In other words, you'll be combining two methods: the ratio method and the drip-feed method.

Let's cover what you'll be doing as far as the ratio method— how many cigarettes should you match with each tablespoon of **Living Silica**?

Start day one with your first five cigarettes. Before each cigarette (or immediately after) take one tablespoon of the Living Silica-Collagen Booster and mix it in a couple ounces of water and drink.

Let the first two cigarettes be paired with a double dose (two tablespoons). Cigarettes three to five are paired with one tablespoon of the Living Silica. That's all. Any further cigarettes just smoke without pairing to the silica.

Now, during that very same day you will have prepared two bottles of "silica water" to sip from every so often during the day. These are your sipping bottles.

So, the first day is a combination of the ratio method (for the first five cigarettes) and the drip-feed method (occassionally sipping on your prepared silica water bottle)

If by the end of the day your cravings have been diminished significantly, then on day two you should be increasing the frequency and/or amounts.

For example, on Day Two: Prepare three sipping water bottles and match six or seven cigarettes with a silica dose. At the end of the day you'll be able to gauge where you are with your cravings and what to do the next day. You should be smoking much less on day two than on day one. If you are not you need to increase frequency or amounts on day three. **This is the exact place where your intuition and judgement come into play.** You are the boss here and you need to decide where to go as far as frequency and amounts per serving.

You can also approach this in a periodic manner. Every two to three hours or so, you can take two tablespoons three to four

time a day. If you notice a significant change, take it five times a day on day two and so forth. Plenty of people have been successful with this way of doing things. It's the most common way, actually. This approach, however, requires diligence in timing— you must be sure to pay attention to the clock so that not too much time passes between doses. If you're sufficiently motivated either method will get you to the goal— the extinction of your cravings for tobacco.

WHAT DID I DO?

I've used all the silica products mentioned above and they're all excellent. But the very first silica supplement that I used was Solgar's Oceanic Silica. It's also the one I still use today. And I still use some Bamboo silica supplements. Both of these, Solgar and bamboo, come in capsule form.

Since this was a new thing the problem I had at the very beginning was, of course, "How much should I take to quell my desires?"

Here's what happened.

I decided to do the three times a day thing— for no other reason than the fact that since time immemorial humans have been dividing the day into the tripartite division of morning, afternoon and night. At this time I was smoking around twenty cigarettes a day.

So day one was one capsule three times. I noticed my cravings did go down. I didn't finish the pack of cigarettes.

The next day I did the thing that I've been trying to tell you throughout this chapter: I took more . . . because I saw it was effective and I surmised that there just might be a specific point, as far as daily silica intake, where the cravings would completely go away.

So . . . on day two I doubled the total amount. I took six capsules total. One capsule every couple of hours. I barely smoked five cigarettes the entire day.

Obviously this was going the right way and I was feeling good. I took eight capsules on day three. I had absolutely no desire to smoke at all that whole day.

Magic number reached! At least for me. I've known more than a few people that needed much more per day from this product, at first.

I stayed with eight capsules for about ten days. Near the end of that ten day period I felt that I didn't need as much silica.

So I went back to six a day. I was getting the same effect–absolutely no desire to smoke–while taking six a day.

Another week or so passed when I decided to take even less. Four capsules a day. Taking four a day was now like taking eight a day when I first started out!

And this is where I'm at now— around three to four capsules a day.

Throughout the years I have experimented at how long I can go without taking silica regularly. Usually it's just a few days before I start craving cigarettes. It also depends on how I'm eating— whether or not I'm eating silica-rich foods or not. But I have fallen off the wagon many times— mostly for the sake of experimentation. But once I start taking silica again the desire almost instantly goes away. This is just all to say that after you hit that pleasant place (where you don't need as much silica and your cravings are a thing of the past) do not let your guard down as far as silica intake.

So these days I un-sleeve the capsules and add the powder to my green drink and shake it up. Twice a day. No cravings. Sometimes I do put them in yogurt. Incidentally, that's the great flexibility of capsules. You can either swallow them whole or take the sleeves off and mix the powder with whatever you want.

Anyway, I don't get cocky anymore and feel I can skip taking silica for a whole week or something. I can for a day or so, but not much more. When I do skip I make sure to make it up by eating more silica-rich foods.

But that's how the whole discovery began. With certain foods.

SILICA IN FOOD

Cucumbers. This silica-rich vegetable is how it all started for me years before I took my first silica supplement. Four cucumbers a day and within a week I was smoke free.

Not really feasible for everyone though, is it? Even if you did love cucumbers, four a day or even two a day is a bit much. But it doesn't hurt to know which foods are high in silica because **it leaves you the option to weave them into your overall silica intake**.

The reason cucumbers are rich in silica is due to the skin. So, obviously, peeling the skin is not going to afford any benefits as far as smoking cessation. The skin is fibrous. Wherever you have fiber in food you have silica, like a mathematical equation, silica=fiber. And fiber=silica.

A high fiber diet would be a good thing but, as mentioned previously, the climate of opinion is not too friendly toward fiber intake and such, but there is actually another reason why higher fiber intake may be the laborious road to smoking cesssation. The strange thing about fiber from rice and grains is that it has a low absorption rate. The content of silica is high but the bioavailability of the silica for your system is surprisingly low. In one study, from the University of Antwerp, oat flakes showed a bioavailabilty rate of only 2.1 percent of the total silicon in the oat flakes. Whole grain rice only had a bioavailabilty rate of 7.6 percent of the total silicon available. Out of the grains, the silica in whole wheat was the most biologically available at 20% availability (not too bad actually). These are foods that are high in silica content yet low in bioavailability! (Silicon in Foods, Harry Robberecht, International Journal of Food Properties 11:638-645)

If these foods were more bioavailable I would be able to write a book about smoking cessation entitled "Eat Your Way to Being Smoke Free".

But because grains have such low bioavailability I can't. You would have to incorporate a great deal of grains into your diet— morning, noon and night. Possible but not that practical. As stated earlier, there is a small percentage of people that have read this book and have gone down that road— successfully.

And I did it. Once. Okay, maybe more than once.

For the sake of experimentation. Please keep that in mind.

After the discovery, I began experimenting with high fiber diets. I decided to use a 'mono' approach. I wanted to see if I could do it with just one grain end-product so I chose a fairly common morning food. I had eight pieces of toast in one day. Sprouted wheat bread (Ezekiel) with a ton of butter on each slice. Two slices at around 7 in the morning. Two slices about three hours later. And then again two slices three hours after that. And two more slices about two hours later. Hey, it was an experiment.

But the fruit of that strange experiment was that I had absolutely no desire to smoke at all by the time I was on the third set of toasts. Great results but I'm sure you can see the undesirability factor in eating eight pieces of toast a day. I did this 'mono-method' with other high fiber grains rich in silica like rice and oat bran. I did the same thing with each— having it throughout the day beginning in the morning. And each one was amazingly capable of preventing my desire to smoke.

But the quantities!

Nevertheless, there have been people that seem to be able to manipulate a shortcoming and create an outlet which circumscribes the shortcoming. In other words, the question that they pose to themselves is How can I get enough fiber in my diet to make me quit smoking and still have it enjoyable? Once you pose the question to your imagination interesting things can happen.

WHAT DID ALICE DO?

Alice didn't like the idea of "pill-popping", as she told me, for her silica needs. So there would be no supplements whatsoever in her routine. She decided to incorporate cucumbers and cucumbers only in her diet. And she wasn't really a big fan of cucumbers!

The way she overcame this shortcoming may look simplistic but I found it rather creative.

Alice's approach after reading my first book? Cucumber smoothies.

She had been smoking a pack a day for 38 years and had tried two common cesssation methods: nicotine replacement and hypnosis (multiple times). Neither of them worked for long. She always found herself having to battle cravings eventually with these methods.

But within one week of her cucumber smoothie adventure, she completely quit. And 5 years later she still incorporates smoothies that are rich in silica into her diet. Pay attention: There was a technique she used that was vital in her quitting which I think you'll find familiar. She intuitively felt that she needed a continuous supply of silica in order to quit. Accordingly she would make a big smoothie and sip away at it rather than having it in one sitting. Then she would make another and do the same thing so that within every hour or so she was getting several hits of silica— all through the day. Sound familiar? That was precisely Zach's method for the Orgono powder in which he loaded his 20 ounce water bottle with one rounded teaspoon of the Orgono Silica Powder and just sipped away for a couple hours— then he would reload and he would do this 4 times per day. And it was also Jon's method during his maintenance phase.

There's a multitude of recipes on the internet that cover this so you can create anything to your heart's desire as long as you emphasize the cucumber as a dominant element in the smoothie. Once again, KEEP THE SKIN INTACT. Make sure the device you're using isn't one of those that disposes with the fiber. The skin, the fiber, is where the silica resides.

A rather fascinating story has to do with a woman who had become pregnant. The problem was she was a long time smoker and she was having difficulty ditching the cigarettes. But she needed to quit and her husband was adamant about her stopping. She came across my first ebook on a website and promptly downloaded it. She was leery about taking a supplement during her pregnancy and she wasn't too crazy about cucumbers either.

She had an idea that I didn't explicitly mention in the book. She did not like cucumbers but she sure loved pickles. And what's a pickle but a fermented cucumber?

Needless to say, her problem was solved because she feasted on pickles every day— as much as she had the desire for. Not only did she stop smoking but her sugar cravings went away and she didn't gain that much weight.

OTHER FOODS

Sprouted wheat cereals are also available that you can have in the morning— maybe right after your supplement? Good idea! A high fiber bran flake cereal can be a good substitute but watch out for sugar content. Try to get the one with the lowest.

Let's not forget about the various oat cereals that are out there.

Whole grain rice? Fantastic. It must be the unhulled or brown rice because— remember? Silica resides in the bran fiber.

Used to having a donut with that coffee? How about a bran muffin or oat/bran muffin instead?

There are creative ways, other than the smoothie, that you can incorporate the cucumber. I found many people making something resembling a dish from Greece known as Tzatziki or something close to it. You dice a cucumber (keep skin on remember?) and also dice a garlic clove and mix them both into a cup of cottage cheese (or even sour cream or yogurt). Let it sit in the refrigerator for about a half hour and you have a rather delicious snack or mini-meal.

These are only a few suggestions that can help you see the world through "silica glasses". You'll be looking at food differently, once you start equating fiber with silica.

Be creative. You can create snacks and recreate foods that you normally eat into silica-rich food. For example you can heighten the amount of silica in that lunch salad you normally have by adding wheat germ flakes.

You can add wheat germ to your yogurt . . . or even add cucumbers.

You can even add the silica capsules to this concoction by unsleeving the capsule and pouring the contents into the mix. Same for the cottage cheese concoction mentioned above. What's great about the bamboo silica capsules and the Oceanic silica capsules is that the contents are virtually tasteless so they mix very well.

Obviously this does not exhaust the variety of things that you can do. Create something that fits your lifestyle. Once you figure out the secret that fiber equals silica then you can just let your imagination flow.

WHAT DID BARRY DO?

My first book emphasized fiber more than this present volume and one of the success stories was a gentleman by the name of Barry. He decided to use the fiber approach exclusively. He smoked a pack of cigarettes daily for almost 15 years and he was, and still is, of average frame and height: 5ft 10in and 170lbs. The reason I bring this last part up is that he is the same exact weight five years later while still maintaining a high fiber diet. Grains that are not fractionated or processed, in the sense of removal of the fibrous portion, cannot and will not contribute to weight gain.

Anyway, here is what Barry did:

In the morning Barry would start his day with a decent sized bowl of sprouted cereal with milk. The name of the brand was Ezekiel. Occassionally he would have other cereals but they all had to be high in fiber and whole wheat or whole grain with minimum sugars.

Sometimes he substituted sprouted wheat toast for the cereal. Two to three pieces with butter.

Between breakfast and lunch Barry would always have a bran muffin with his coffee during the morning hours. Again, no sugar sprinkles or any thing of the sort added to it. Just a high fiber bran muffin.

For lunch Barry always ate two to three whole pickles with his sandwich.

In the hours between lunch and dinner, Barry's favorite high fiber snack was yogurt with a generous serving of **nutritional yeast flakes** mixed together. There are so many brands of this product that even Barry switched often, simply for variety in taste. One of the main ones that he uses is from a company called **Sari**. A favorite of mine was by a company called **KAL**. Still another one is **Anthony's**. But there are simply too many to list and they all have their own unique, delicious taste.

For dinner, most everyone has something that they didn't have the day before. It's not feasible to make every dinner a high silica meal but pretty much most dinners can make room for a salad and so adding a little extra cucumber to your salad is a good thing. This is what Barry did most of the time.

In the hours before bedtime, Barry always made a silica-rich treat which consisted of coconut milk (comes in a can from your local market) a tablespoon or two of blackstrap molasses and a few tablespoons of the nutritional yeast flakes. He mixed these together in a blender and a delicious treat was the outcome. Again, this was a high fiber snack because of the nutritional yeast flakes.

So how long did it take for Barry to quit on this high fiber diet? After one week on this diet Barry could only manage half a pack of cigarettes daily. But he really wasn't enjoying those either. After three weeks Barry dropped his cigarettes altogether.

Now you might call this the turtle method but to Barry it was quite easy and painless and he still got to where he wanted to be which was smoke-free. During those three weeks he smoked whenever he wanted and thoroughly enjoyed his diet.

The take-away from this is that quitting smoking can be done without supplements but it may be a little slower for various reasons.

Now that we've covered two general approaches–food and supplements– to smoking cessation we can now cover the great synthesis. Supplements and food combined can be the most effective path to remain smoke-free forever.

A SILICA DAY

Now you have all the practical directions for complete success. The next step is the application of these directions and that is going to take some thinking. And creativity. You have the choice of 'cut and paste' or you can concoct something on your own, blending different elements from the examples. There's nothing wrong with simply copying an example from the previous pages— cut and paste. Most people do this and it works. But sometimes a person might hit an obstacle and may need to change things around. An example would be some of the people that read the book wanted to do 'food only' but could not keep it up because of unforeseen hurdles in their schedule. They had good intentions but what inevitably happened was they found themselves constrained to adopt a sort of hybrid method of 'food *and* supplements'. Nothing wrong with that at all. As long as you look at each day as a "silica day"— always keeping in mind the question "When was the last time I took silica?" This mindfulness, this awareness, will make you successful right from the start.

If you treat this process as a "side-thing" and secondary, almost as a diversion, then it will not yield results. There must be an appreciation for the fact that you are in a state of starvation— for a specific nutrient. If you neglect this state of stravation you will only maintain the hunger state and you will still feel cravings.

Come up with a plan and be vigilant over your intake. Be relentless.

Brenda did just that.

1. Upon waking up (7 A.M.) she took two capsules of a bamboo based silica and one niacin tablet of 100mg

2. One hour later (8 A.M.) she was eating two pieces of sprouted wheat bread (toasted) with butter.

3. At 9 A.M. she took two more of the bamboo silica capsules.

4. At 10 AM she had a pickle for a snack.

5. At precisely 11 A.M. she took two capsules of the bamboo silica along with 1 tablet of niacin 100 mg.

Are you seeing it? The regularity, that is? Every hour upon the hour Brenda was making sure that she was having a silica source. She really took that principle to heart and it was working. By lunch time the cigarettes were tasting aweful and she only had smoked two whereas her usual number was four or five smoked cigarettes by noon. Let's continue.

At lunch (12 P.M.) Brenda had a cucumber salad with extra cucumbers.

At 1 P.M. she took one capsule of the bamboo silica.

At 2 P.M. she did the same along with 1 tablet of niacin 100 mg.

At 3 P.M. she mixed in two of the silica capsules (by pulling apart the sleeves) with her small yogurt for a snack.

At 4 P.M. one silica capsule.

At 5 P.M she took one silica capsule along with 1 tablet of niacin 100 mg.

At 6:30 she had her dinner with a side salad that had a generous portion of cucumbers.

At 9 P.M. she had her last silica capsule and soon after went to bed.

The final tally of cigarettes smoked was 6, of which the last 3 were not smoked completely. She ordinarily smoked a pack a day (20 cigarettes)

This is a pretty good examle of blending food and supplements. She was a bit more reliant on the supplements but that's perfectly okay. Observe that she kept an hourly schedule. I want you to note that because the very next day she kept the same exact schedule except for one thing— whenever she would smoke she would take an additional capsule.

In other words, she mixed two methods— the ratio method and the periodic method. She kept to her hourly schedule but if she wanted to smoke at 10:30 AM (which was off from her hourly schedule) she would take an additional silica capsule before she smoked. And this brought her to three cigarettes.

The third day she simply had no desire to smoke.

Obviously, you can substitute any silica supplement. Especially if you want to be sure of absorption you can start with monomethylsilanetriol, the most digestible form mentioned in the previous pages.

Be creative and always be asking yourself (at least in the beginning) "When was the last time I had silica?"

SMOKING IS HISTORY

Go back over the material in this chapter. Come up with your own plan or follow one of the examples note for note. Remember, do not try to stop smoking. It will come easily and naturally, once you find the right amount of silica and the frequency you should be taking it. Once this happens an amazing phenomenon will take place— you're desires for tobacco will completely vanish. You'll regard this mineral as the 'magic' mineral, indeed.

I'm very much interested in your testimony and any questions that you might have. Keep this in mind . . . the situations and questions that people had in the past regarding the principles in this book have helped many today in the present. That means your testimony and/or question will help someone in the future. Drop a line at

paracelsuspress@gmail.com

A POSTSCRIPT *NAM ILUSTRATIO*

If you've read this far solely for the practical information then you don't have to proceed any further. The following pages are strictly for enlightenment, a sort of 'rounding out' of the story that was begun in the Introduction with the parable of the peel-eaters. You can go directly to the next chapter if you wish.

HOW TO QUIT . . . THE WRONG WAY

There are only two ways to quit smoking. The good way and the bad way. What is fascinating is that they both involve silica. If you've read this far, especially chapters two and three, then what is coming up will not be a shock.

The thing that distinguishes one way from the other is the *carrier* of silica. If silica is reintroduced into your diet by way of foods and/or supplements naturally high in silica then you will quit smoking quite easily and not have any side effects.

But silica can also be gotten through bad sources known as non-foods. Remember chapters two and three with the phenomenon known as pica? Remember the various pica objects that people used as a pica source and still use? What are they all seeking? Silica. The very next chapter will show exactly how silica is in every pica object. Everyone who tries to quit smoking, and anyone in history who has ever tried to quit, must replace their silica source from tobacco with another source and usually the choice is for the worst silica source– refined sugar. Sugar is the ultimate non-food and as such the most dangerous.

The reason for sugar being less than desirable is that it will cause inflammation which will lead to physical and mental deterioration

1) weight gain initially and inflammatory physical diseases long-term

2) mental problems

One of the underlying principles explicated throughout this book, especially chapters one through three, is the principle of reorientation: *If you try to quit smoking cigarettes your body, especially the brain, cannot quit silica. When you stop smoking, your body will turn on the "silica detector switch" and acquire silica in another form somewhere else in the environment (chapter three).* This is the missing piece of knowledge that makes all the difference in your pursuit to quit smoking. The reason that switch is turned on is because silica, as demonstrated in the last chapter, is a major player in brain function. If you stop providing silica from that cigarette, your body will go into a mode to 'discover' silica in another form in your environment. This concept of *reorientation* from chapter one and also the Introduction concerning the peel-eaters is a good thing to review. In this regard, keep in mind the examples of people from chapter two who were eating clay and laundry detergent and other such nonfoods in their mode of reorientation. As stated, the next chapter will show that these non-foods and every other pica object is actually a *container* for silica!

So now the picture should be forming in your mind— the human body has an absolute dependence on this mineral like no other nutrient or element except maybe oxygen. It is exquisitely designed in that it even has an emergency plan to acquire this mineral when it is scarce in the regular food supply. These 'acquisitions', obtaining pica objects (tobacco being one of them), are not ideal of course in the long run— but they do serve the highly important purpose of providing silica short-term.

In other words, you may invoke willpower and go 'cold turkey' when you try to quit smoking but your body has its own way of thinking because it *must* have silica and it makes an 'adjustment' in order to acquire this mineral in some other 'container'— whether food or nonfood. So, for most, the story goes like this: there you are, a few years later after quitting, proud to tell everyone how you did it through brute willpower and, though you have those extra twenty pounds and are on some pharmaceuticals for your depression, you've convinced yourself and others that it was well worth it.

This sums up many 'successful' quitters. Is this you?

However, there are people out there that have, perhaps unwittingly, quit smoking the proper way with proper diet and such but it seems to be the exception rather than the norm. What most likely happens is that the former smoker will choose a *silica container* that is ubiquitous and convenient— none other than *refined sugar*.

'Wait', you may be saying, 'sugar has silica in it?'

Amazingly, as will be shown in the next chapter, sugar has a residue of silica in it. In fact, silica is even added into sugar by manufacturers and approved by the World Health Organization as such for certain purposes as the next chapter will show.

Here is a fundamental principle of Smoking Cessation 101 in regard to sugar. Remember this:

The problem with choosing sugar (you don't consciously choose it, your body does) when you stop smoking is that you will need to consume *much more* sugar to equal the concentrated silica delivered by means of smoke/particulate from tobacco. And we all know what happens to people when they increase their sugar intake. They get fat.

You are not chewing on that candy bar to "have something to do". You are not bored and have an 'oral fixation'. That is fiction (see chapter nine on 'oral fixation' fraud). What is actually the case is that your body (and brain) is starving for a specific mineral— silica—and it is seeking it out in another form which is in the sugar in that candy bar or soda.

Even refined grains, though most of the silica is removed, still contain a residue. Again, because it is in smaller amounts and less bioavailable forms, you must *eat more* to get the same result you would get from obtaining silica from a cigarette. So what happens then? More weight gain.

This all leads us to a gentleman who wrote a very popular book about how "easy" it was to quit smoking. However, over the years this book misled millions of people into thinking that smoking was a psychological issue rather than what it really is: a physiological response to special-hunger. But let's look at what happened as a result of that book which misled many. The ultimate outcome was that people got fat and/or depressed. Curiously, another book was released shortly after the "easy" quit smoking book— by the same gentleman. This time it had to do with how "easy" it was to lose weight.

Why did the "easy" weight-loss book follow on the heels of the popular "easy" smoking book?

The answer is clear if you've read this far. People didn't understand at the time (or even now) that even if they got hypnotized by a book or a person or even exerted their will, that their body was going to turn to an alternative silica source regardless of their choice of gimmick for quitting. As a result the world got heavier. You're duped into thinking you have a choice in this matter. You can not fight your body's hunger and need for silica. Your body will always seek an alternative source for silica and it most likely will turn out to be sugar because of its ubiquity in our society. When sugar is not available people will turn to other sources of silica (see chapter two). The same principle applies today. Much like gravity it is very difficult to disobey the laws of hunger.

The general point is this: You need silica and vitamin B3 not only to quit smoking but also for proper brain functioning as shown in the previus two chapters. When silica is removed by a societal decision or a personal decision there will be physical and psychic repercussions and the pharmaceutical industry will swoop right in to fill the gap.

A STRANGE THING HAPPENED IN THE EIGHTIES

Remember the parable of the peel-eaters from the introduction? That story was meant to demonstrate one of the central truths of this book: A vital nutrient has been refined out of our food supply just like the peel-eaters discovered on their own world. Then another central truth was demonstrated: Once the peel-eaters discovered that the missing nutrient was the *cause* of their reorientation to a nonfood (see chapter one for *reorientation*), they began incorporating the missing nutrient back into their diet and their pica problem, peel-eating, magically disappeared.

On planet earth, the pica problem of cigarette smoking can disappear once the missing nutrient(s) is put back into the regular diet of earthlings.

What is the missing nutrient that has been removed by mass refining? Silica. And fiber is the main foodstuff that is the main container for silica. But I ask you, Where is fiber in the American diet?

Let's think a moment about the late 19th and all of the 20th century (even the 21st) when it comes to fiber.

On planet earth what food or food group was refined to the point that silica was removed and nonexistent in our diet? Or, now that we have wisdom, we can ask what heavily refined food was it that initially forced our civilization to search out silica in the nonfood of tobacco?

We're going to go down a little side-road to answer this question.

In the mid to late eighties of the twentieth century people began doing a very strange thing. If you were old enough at the time you would have noticed it or maybe even participated in it. It seemed that wherever you turned, people were stuffing bran muffins in their faces. A fad had hit the nation and every day millions of Americans religiously began their day consuming bran muffins while downing their cups of coffee. Media outlets could hardly ignore it. The New York Times wrote about this sensation a few times but at one point in 1988 there was an article called *Oat Bran: The Muffin And the Mania* in which the owner of a local take-out business boasted that the demand for bran muffins was so great that "he could charge anything he wanted for it." The writer of the article goes on to say that, "Nothing, not even calcium pills, has roused such interest among a public that is constantly searching for a simple route to perfect health." There was no doubt about it, bran was *in*. But why?

Doctors, health practitioners, commercials on tv, ads in newspapers— everyone was encouraging the increase of fiber intake. Studies were showing that it lowered cholesterol and therefore it was heart healthy. So said the authorities. And oat bran being high in fiber, the humble bran muffin, almost overnight, became a fixture in American diets.

In reality there was a gradual building up to this moment because in the early seventies scientists and researchers like Dr. Denis Burkitt, from his work in rural Africa, were discovering (rediscovering) the benefits of fiber in the human diet. It was a slow burn, in some sense, that needed the kindling of the oat bran studies in the eighties (which attributed the benefits of oat bran to the greater content of soluble fiber). The conjunction of the two streams was brought to light by the media and in popular books which touted fiber as being the cure-all for disease. In short, by the late eighties the whole focus of the world changed. From early morning to late at night people were genuinely concerned with fiber intake and becoming more "regular". In the morning people had bran muffins with their coffee. At lunch and dinner, people were worried about whether the bread or pasta was 'whole grain' or not. And then for snacks people would have another bran muffin. I was even a witness to this craze. It was, at least in America, a national phenomenon.

And then it happened . . . if you were paying attention.

Many of these very same bran and fiber fanatics were suddenly quitting smoking with incredible ease.

What were they doing right?

Everyone that quit smoking claimed that it was old-fashioned willpower. Or was it?

For successful quitters the decision to quit came first and the diet change came second. There was seemingly no connection between the two. The one was as far away from the other as the east is from the west.

But there was/is a connection between a high fiber diet and smoking cessation. Fiber (from grains, fruits, vegetables), as established in the last chapter, happens to be a container for silica. In fact, in a human dietary sense, it is *the* source for silica. This is the principal reason why fiber is good for you— because it has silica. And this is the principal reason why those people in the eighties stopped smoking so easily. And, what's fascinating is that this is about the time that the "easy" book for quitting came out. Were people reading that book quitting because of advice from the book, or from certain eating patterns?

Anyway, despite this small episode of higher fiber intake in the eighties and early nineties, there remained the overwhelming ironic tragedy of the rest of the 20th century: The rich silica source known as fiber was practically nonexistent in the 20th century. Fiber was removed from grain end-products— leaving white bread, white rice, white pasta, white sugar, etc. Silica was 'missing-in-action' from the human diet and hardly to return except through fads.

This book has documented what the human organism does in times of scarcity so here's the gist of the matter. Again. When the human body misses out on silica intake it will *reorient* itself toward alternative food sources or nonfood sources as was established in chapter one. This sophisticated switch that the body turns on will seek out and obtain silica in the environment even if it is in a nonfood source (see chapter two). And this is precisely what the whole world did in the 20th century. That nonfood source for silica was sought out and found and readily available. This source was none other than tobacco.

And the whole world began smoking.

CHAPTER 7: PICA SOLVED!

Silica is the common denominator in every pica object no matter how diverse they may seem. Whether it is ice cubes or clay or refined sugar or chalk or charcoal or tobacco, silica is in the composition of these items in some quantity or form. The cell has a single minded purpose in seeking this element and, as this book has shown, it will hurdle taste or convention in order to obtain it. Silica is all around us but it is in forms that are not dietary.

VARIETIES OF SILICA

Clay and dirt contain silica. Only a few plants are considered heavy accumulators of silica but it is readily available in the ground— besides oxygen it is the most abundant element in the earth's crust. At the molecular level even though other minerals are there, silica forms sheets interspersed with other sheets of magnesium or aluminum that form a sort of 'sandwich'. Some clays form a three layer sandwich at the molecular level with silica as the 'bread' layers, while the other mineral sheet resides in the middle.

Two common pica substances, even to this day, are laundry starch and cornstarch. Laundry detergent has a component to it called a 'builder'. Builders are designed to 'soften water' because hard water, which is a concentration of minerals, interferes with the cleaning action of the detergent. Builders take up the majority of the weight in a detergent upwards of 50 percent. A common builder that is added to laundry detergent is called zeolite. What is interesting is that zeolites are alumino*silicate* minerals. Aluminosilicates are composed of oxygen, aluminum and of course . . . silica. Even before zeolites were added to detergents there was usually some form of silicate in detergent in order to soften the water. An example, for instance, comes from Germany where the Henkel company developed and marketed their famous 'universal detergent' in the late 19th century—this detergent was silicate based.

Corn starch has a residue of silica in it that the processing has not fully removed. The bran layer of the kernel of corn is rich in silica. Though the layer is removed in the refining stages there is a residue that is left behind that cannot be fully removed in the refining process. Also, the amylopectin of the starch is probably where this residue is hiding. This has not been confirmed but the crystalline structure of these glucose chains must be due to silica.

Glass, believe it or not, is a substance of pica even though it is not as commonly reported. I am not talking about circus sideshows but real individuals who have this problem. The *Journal of Neuropsychiatry and Clinical Neurosciences* (2013;25:E46-E48) states that it is not as commonly known "due to underreporting to embarrassed patients." In an article in that particular issue entitled, *The Behavior of Eating Glass, With Radiological Findings: A Case of Pica*, Dr. Kumsar, the author, writes about a 32 year old male who had been consuming glass on a regular basis for 10 years. "We learned that the patient . . . constantly keeps glass pieces in his mouth during the day, chews and swallows them, feels restlessness and irritability whenever he does not have them, and embarks on a quest; this behavior of quest gradually increases with this craving." This is the same thing that cigarette smokers go through and the body reorients itself on this 'quest', as the doctor called it— which is actually reorientation. During the day the patient would experience certain times when he felt more stress or anxiety but eating the glass would calm him down— just like a cigarette does. "It was determined that the patient had some anxiety periods during the day, which showed fluctuations and could not be associated with any reason. He stated that the eating of glass generally increased in these periods, and he felt relief." This one is fairly easy, for we know that the composition of glass is quartz or sand, therefore silica. Beware— if a culture or an individual has a firm belief that cigarette smoking is bad or immoral this can't trick the body. The cells of the brain and body need silica and will go on a 'quest' to obtain it one way or the other.

Chalk is a common item of pica. Chalk is composed of limestone and gypsum, both of which have silica naturally interspersed through out them.

Charcoal, matches and ashes all have residue of silica in them. Remember how the xylem of a tree is composed of silica— the charcoal still retains a skeletal structure which is mainly composed of silica.

SMOKING METAL

It may be difficult to conceive of humans eating these things on a regular basis but if we understand the basic underlying physiology of silica function, how it puts out the fire, then we know the cell has an intensive need for this mineral that will conscript the body in order to obtain it, wherever it is.

This next one is one of the more challenging ones to fathom but it seems to pop up in the press from time to time. One example is from February 18 of 2004 in which it was reported by the Associated Press that a 62 year old man, who had stomach pain and could not move his bowels, went to the hospital for his problem. Upon x-raying the patient the doctors found a– what turned out to be– twelve pound mass in his stomach that was causing the stomach to droop down between his hips internally. This was strange enough but when the doctors proceeded to remove the mass they were in for a bigger surprise. The 'mystery mass' consisted of coins, assorted jewelry, and needles— yes, needles. It was also reported that the man had a history of major mental illness but it was not clear if he was currently (at the time) recovered from this. If you have read this book from the beginning you understand that consuming partial-foods, over a long period of time, stripped of silica and other nutrients, can cause mental illness— which is really a form of inflammation. To alleviate the situation the individual will engage on a 'quest' for silica even though it may be in nonfood forms. If the individual does come across a form of silica and takes it in the right amounts the problem—mental or bodily illness— may go away. The only thing is, though, that the form of silica may not be really all that healthy long term. This becomes more clear when we look at the next case which also involved a patient with mental illness but with an interesting twist, as we shall see.

This was reported in the *Journal of Geriatric Psychiatry*, September 1998; the title of the article was called *An Unusual Case of Pica*. It involved a 72 year old woman who, " . . at emergency laparotomy, had 175.32 Pounds of loose change in her stomach." What is interesting with this case is that the woman had, at one point in her life, schizophrenia but according to the article, ". . . she had had no positive symptoms of schizophrenia for at least 20 years." Up until this emergency operation the woman was free of mental illness and had been for 20 years. Why is this significant? In the same article the writer states that the woman had engaged in pica for the last 20 years! The connection is not made, however, between the fact that the symptoms of mental illness went away when the woman started ingesting the coins that contained silica— which put out the fire in the brain of this schizophrenic.

Now these two cases involve coins which seemingly, at the outset, have nothing to do with silica— which would seem to lead us away from our hypothesis. However, copper is the majority element in coins and copper ore consists of many other metals including a good amount of silicon. In the smelting process it is mixed with coke and sand (silica). Though silica is almost entirely removed in high electrical grade copper, the copper used for coins is not as purified as the copper used for high electrical conductivity— so coins still contain a residue of silicon.

Another case of pica that was reported in a medical journal involved a young woman who ate iron nails. Upon investigation, it was found that the 27 year old was under a great deal of stress from her traditional parents who wanted her to marry a certain man while the woman was actually carrying on an affair wth another person. This led her to ingest nails regularly. The psychologists that reported this in the *Indian Journal of Psychological Medicine* (2011 volume 3) of course, being psychologists, explained it in psychological terms. They state that the eating of the iron nails, " . . may have been an act to depict her 'bravery' whenever she felt an essence of hopelessness and failure in her real life." Again, in the stressful state that she was in, she needed silica. But how is it in iron nails? This is from the on-line encyclopedia Wikipedia concerning iron ore: "Silica ($SiO2$) is almost always present in iron ore . . . At temperatures above 1300 °C some will be reduced and form an alloy with the iron. The hotter the furnace, the more silicon will be present in the iron."

Also, any pica that has to do with steel is dealing with a certain amount of silica. There is even a class of steels known as silicon steel because of their higher than normal silica amount which is up to 15%.

SMOKING ICE

Well, what about ice and ice cubes? Before we delve into this we must understand a basic principle of biochemistry: Everything that we eat has shape or geometry. I am not talking about the shape of the food on your plate but at the molecular level. A molecule of water has a shape in three dimensional space that distinguishes it from other molecules. Amino acids and peptide chains can have great complexity and intricate shapes that are important to their *function*. These amino acids, for instance, form bigger entities such as peptide chains and proteins which have specific shapes which in turn have specific functions due to that shape. So we could say that, at the molecular level, *shape determines function*. Did you get that? In fact, when an amino acid is rearranged so that it bends light a different way than in its natural form, it is rendered biologically useless in most cases though it has the *same* chemical formula. These isomers or mirror images of the amino have the same chemistry as their counter part but can not have the same function . . . all due to shape.

The elements from the periodic table also have distinct shapes. But rarely are the elements found in their pure state. The element Silicon, for instance, is found in nature bound up with another element known as Oxygen; these two form silica or silicon dioxide which has a distinct geometrical shape. The tetrahedral shape of the silica molecules arrange themselves through their vertices into a *hexagonal* structure repeated over and over again in a lattice like network. When water freezes, the crystalline structure of the ice crystals are of an hexagonal dipyramidal form . . . the same form as silica. The geometry of the ice *mimics* silica. If anyone doubts this, all you have to do is give silica to an individual who craves ice . . . the craving will go away. Be sure to give them the most absorbable silica you can, as mentioned in chapter six. Also, if anyone doubts this in general, just keep in mind the geometric nature of the molecular world. There is more to this subject of geometry and energy that is beyond the scope of this book. The Russian scientist Nikolai Kozyrev made some interesting headway in this direction as did the Czech researcher Robert Pavlita.

THE GREATEST OF THEM ALL

A person may quit smoking but they can never quit silica. The body must have some form of silica. So when a person quits smoking the body reorients to another form. The form that is most chosen in our modern age is sugar. This is the form that is A) readily available in our society and B) the cause of all our modern pathologies (because it is isolated) whether mental or physical as this book has shown.

We may not be eating sweets because of their sweetness but because of some other factor— mainly the fact that sugar contains silica. And just like with any other pica object, it is not the ideal form of silica for our diet (chapter 2 and 3)

That silica is part of refined sugar is acknowledged in all the textbooks of the sugar cane processing industry and in their published papers. In the 2004 SASTA (South African Sugar Technologists' Association) annual publication, one of the papers is entitled *Aspects of the Effects of Silica During Cane Sugar Processing*. The problem for the authors, which is a problem for the sugar industry in general, is that too much silica can interfere with the manufacturing process. As the authors state at the beginning of the article, "Silica is a major component of soil and an essential element for the sugarcane plant." So it is naturally in the plant but there are additional sources, say the authors, that contaminate the process of refining. "There is, however, evidence of contamination from soil and clay, entering the mill with the cane. This contamination could add relatively large quantities of silica . . ." the authors state there is even another source from the refining process which is dependent on lime, ". . . lime can contain much soluble silica, which is then transferred to the juice."

In fact, the sugarcane plant absorbs many minerals for its growth but the one it absorbs the most is silicon. If it were not refined, and the vitamins and other minerals were left intact, the sugarcane plant would indeed be a superfood for health and fitness but this is not the case today. All the minerals and vitamins are refined and boiled off and then re-sold as blackstrap molasses.

But here is what is most important. In the refining process most of the silica is removed but then *re-added* as an anti-caking agent. In all the refined sugar grades whether ICUMSA

45 or 100 or even 150, the common denominator is silica in some form as an anti-caking agent. The most highly refined sugar is ICUMSA 45. The technical specifications sheet for this grade of sugar, endorsed and set by the World Food Program of the United Nations, lists seven anti-caking agents that are allowed in this grade and five of them are silica based.(Technical Specs for ICUMSA 45)

Ultimately, the problem with sugar as a pica source is that it is not a rich source of silica so that far more of it must be consumed in order for it to "work". This is bad. If you've read this far you know that overconsumption of sugar leads to chronic inflammation and disease. When a smoker quits, more likely than not the common complaint is weight gain and how they seem to be constantly snacking. A constant source of silica is needed and if sugar is chosen then you will eventually get the bad side-effects from it. Thus begins the "spiral" out of which it can be most difficult to reverse. The only way the spiral can be reversed is if you substitute silica rich supplements and/or foods

This mineral has been taken out of the food supply by processing techniques which remove the fibrous element from grains and by fad diets such as paleo and Atkins, etc. which dismiss it out of hand due to a failure to make distinctions. The fibrous part of grain contains vital silica, which is a balancer, an equalizer, an effective manager of the pH environment of the brain. It is to our detriment that we do not incorporate it into our diet. As shown in chapter three, the effects of the deficit of this mineral in our diet resounds in our bodies, our minds, and in our world.

CHAPTER 8: REVELATIONS

The language of myth is very old and there is barely a culture or civilization that doesn't have a mythos. But what is just now beginning to be understood by scholars is that there is more to this phenomenon than meets the eye.

In the Socratic dialogue Timaeus, written by the philosopher Plato over two thousand years ago, we are given some fascinating information about myth and mythology. We are told, in essence, that to take a myth on its face value is incorrect because myth is *representational of a hidden knowledge system.*

Plato tells us, through the mouth of an Egyptian priest, that mythology is not what it seems– a fanciful story about fanciful places, people and events. The priest gives us an example to demonstrate what is actually going on with mythology by using the myth of Phaethon. He tells his listener, the Athenian statesman Solon, that the myth was not just a story for entertainment's sake; instead, he says the story "has the form of myth, but really signifies a declination of the bodies moving in the heavens around the earth, and a great conflagration of things upon the earth which recurs after long intervals . . ."

In other words, the myth is representational of a knowledge system; specifically, in this case, astronomy and history because the myth of Phaethon was symbolizing an actual astro-historical event. Giorgio de Santillana, the historian and philosopher of science, who was professor at MIT, wrote about this phenomenon in his book *Hamlet's Mill*. As he explains: "Cosmic phenomena and rules were articulated in the language, or terminology, of myth, where each key word was at least as "dark" as the equations and convergent series by means of which our modern scientific grammar is built up." (Hamlet's Mill pg.58)

If this is true then we have been disregarding a knowledge system that is right in front of our proverbial noses. What if all of mythology is really a symbolic mode of communicating scientific knowledge? And what in the world does this have to do with tobacco? Everything, as we shall soon see.

MY BROTHER, TOBACCO

In January of 1985 Ken Cohen, the renowned health and Qigong educator, wrote an article for the Yoga Journal about the properties of quartz in healing. The article relates fascinating characteristics of quartz taken from North American Indian mythology. Many such articles have been written in this vein but Cohen had a rather unusual source for his information.

It seems the mythology involving quartz was widely known but kept secret for some reason or other . . . that is, until the medicine man Keetoowah, the 'crystal grandfather', authorized Ken Cohen to write about quartz in his article. Keetoowah was well versed in the sacred Cherokee tradition and Cohen was under his tutelage for nearly 10 years. This particular myth should interest us because it identifies quartz with the plant that we know as tobacco. And we should know by now that quartz is crystal silica.

The myth that Keetoowah reveals deals with the 'Fall' of

man from his former state of glory. According to the myth, mankind turned to evil at some time in the past. Because of this evil inclination in man, the plant, animal, and rock kingdom called a conference to deal with the new evil order of things. This evil impulse in man had to be checked in some way because it would surely get out of control and destroy the whole world.

The Bear tribe, which represented the animal kingdom, proposed bringing disease into the world. This would humble man and shorten his time on earth. But the Plant tribe felt that this was throwing the baby out with the bathwater and so they stepped in by saying that if this were to be so then they would lessen man's pain on earth by being used as remedies. However, one plant spoke louder than the rest and took the stage by saying, "I will be the sacred herb and help people return to the sacred way of life . . ." This was none other than the tobacco plant.

Now for the interesting part. It turns out that the Plant tribe had an ally to help mankind battle disease and that is the Rock and Mineral Tribe. Through their special powers each rock or mineral would have a specific ailment to treat. But the Chief of the Rock tribe was quartz or as we know it, silica. And here is where it gets illuminating.

According to the medicine man Keetoowah, "The Quartz crystal put his arm around *his brother tobacco* and said, "I will be the sacred mineral." (italics mine) There is a family relationship between this rock and plant; seemingly two disparate entities. What could possibly be the relation between the two? But as this book has shown and modern science has proven, tobacco is in fact a silica accumulator. It is really a silica delivery plant. Not only is the term 'brother' a hint but both of them have leadership positions that are similar. For instance, 'I will be the sacred herb' and 'I will be the sacred mineral' connote the same level of ability or function. Seems like some long lost scientific knowledge had been encoded in this myth. But this identification between the two is not all.

ANCIENT SCIENCE

In this book I have taken pains to show that silica is necessary for not only structural formation of bone, skin and teeth but it is also important in function. The neurotransmitters of the brain need a favorable environment to transmit and when this fluid environment becomes unfriendly to transmission, or overly acidic, then the transmitters have difficulty in firing. When this happens then the imprecise calcium/enzyme management system comes in to rectify the situation. This management system is meant to be short term, however, and not long term. When it becomes long term, it causes more problems than it initially solved.

Silica is the mineral of water and oxygen management. These two elements are what the brain needs for proper function. Silica ensures that the surrounding pH in the brain will be optimal because of its almost Magical abilities in directing water and oxygen where they are needed. Because of this ability it truly is a mineral for the mind. And this is exactly what comes through in the Indian myths. Immediately after quartz puts his arm around tobacco and declares him a brother he states that he will be called the sacred mineral but, amazingly he adds, " I will heal the mind." The full text recorded from the utterance of Keetoowah goes like this: "I will be the sacred mineral. I will heal the mind. I will help human beings see the origin of disease. I will help to bring wisdom and clarity in dreams. And

I will record their spiritual history . . ."

Even in this myth we have an association between silica and the mind. Silica does, in a sense, heal the mind if we hold to the picture of Fire and Water that I have painted elsewhere in this book. The Fire is incomplete metabolism of foods thereby causing inflammation (fire) and the Water is silica which rectifies this by drawing or attracting water (and oxygen) to wherever it is.

Remember, the concentrated areas of silica in the brain appear to be associated with memory. Is this why the myth uses such terms as 'wisdom' and 'clarity'? Also, it is interesting that just as in the world of computers, silica seems to have a strange capability, according to the myth, to *record*. "I will *record* their spiritual history . . .", says the quartz crystal. Is this because in the brain, regarding memory and in computers regarding the same thing, that silica is necessary as a substratum to lay down an imprint of information that becomes known as memory?

Can this have something to do with modern mental diseases such as Alzheimers? Remember what silica said— 'I will heal the mind.' From what modern researchers are beginning to understand, there seems to be a heavy metal toxicity in the brain due to excessive aluminum. But why is this occurring? Is it simply an extraneous input due to environmental pollution or something else? Many pots and pans that we use to cook food in may be aluminum based and even many under-arm deodorants have an aluminum content as well as drinking water due to pollution. There definitely is more aluminum in our environment. However, as alluded to in chapter five the main problem of excessive aluminum, is due to metabolism of refined sugars and carbs which create an acid environment— the FIRE. When the acidity of inflammation (from partial-foods consumption) becomes excessive at the cellular level, aluminum is mobilized— it is dissolved into solution. The ratio of aluminum to silica becomes greater and this excessive amount may be the catalyst which causes silica to be 'pushed' out. Silica does not react to the acidic environment caused by poor diet but rather it is aluminum which does— more of it is mobilized. And when more does become mobilized, it bumps off silica, so to speak, which is needed for brain function. Indirectly, silica is removed from important structures due to an acid environment. The same situation is mimicked in nature when acid rain mobilizes aluminum from the ground into solution, thereby causing aluminum polluted water, as I stated in chapter five. So it is not necessarily only an environmental pollution problem that causes excessive aluminum but a dietary one when it comes to the aluminum/silica ratio— acid causes this ratio to become imbalanced and distorted. Less silica in the brain structure will actually translate to less memory capacity and, eventually, loss of cognitive function. This is why, I believe, smoking has been shown to mitigate against cognitive brain disorders such as Alzheimer's and dementia in general.

Final Summary: When silica is not present in the diet the human cell goes into a desperation mode and, if not soon provided, will obtain this precious mineral in a nonfood form. This has been known traditionally as pica and in the last century this nonfood form of obtaining silica has been predominantly through tobacco smoking. The Indian myths were the key in unlocking this enigma of cigarette smoking.

CHAPTER 9: VAPING IS STARVATION

Chances are that if you ask a vaper, they may just tell you— vaping is 'working' for them. Studies seem to point in this direction. A recent study published in February of 2019 concluded that *'E-cigarettes were more effective for smoking cessation than nicotine-replacement therapy'*– (N Engl J Med 2019; 380:629-637). The successful cesssation rate after one year of use was about 18% for vapers while the best that NRT (nicotine replacement therapy) could do was 9%. Historically, that's about the best that NRT has done in studies. This and other studies show that vapers have the edge when trying to quit smoking. And it helps that, relatively speaking, most authorities agree that ecigarettes are still not as harmful as tobacco cigarettes.

The success rate is still way too low for it to be touted as the long sought for cure that will work for everyone— but even a cursory look into the matter reveals a phenomenon that is unlike other cessation modalities. The forums and message boards reveal this. Wheezing and coughing seem to magically disappear. New vapers even report an increase in energy. Most don't put on weight, and if they do it's no way near to the extent of those undergoing NRT or other cessation therapies. And let's not forget the most important thing— many of them *maintain* their cessation from cigarettes.

An 18% success rate is no way near perfect but it's better than what NRT was offering.

It seems like many of these former smokers have finally found a panacea for their bugaboo.

Or have they?

A CONUNDRUM

Ecigarettes are a relatively new thing. As a result the research is somewhat thin in certain aspects. Most of the studies published on vaping and ecig use concentrate on two areas:

1) Are they *safe*?

2) and are they *effective* in smoking cessation?

So it was interesting when a study out of Rutgers medical school fastened on a new aspect of the ecig phenomenon.

According to the study (Nicotine & Tobacco Research, Published: 23 April 2019), it seems that most vapers actually *want to quit vaping*. "Nearly two-thirds of e-cigarette users (1,771 participants) reported plans to quit e-cigarettes for good". Wait a minute. This thing seems to be working better than NRT and other cessation methods, yet people want to get out?

The thing is, more studies are coming out that are pointing out that ecigs may not be so healthy after all. Even though they may be a safer choice than cigarettes there still may be some hidden health risk from certain contaminants. At least that's what the studies are starting to show. What the ultimate risk is can't be fully articulated until time passes. So we can appreciate the fact that vapers are feeling a bit on edge. The initial exuberancy is starting to fade.

But how on earth are these vapers going to quit now, since NRT products failed them before? This brings us to the strange part of the study. Of the sample participants, "over 25% tried to quit in the last year with a majority of them using FDA approved methods such as NRT and FDA approved medication."

What is going on here? Vapers starting to use NRT to get off vaping? Why weren't they using the NRT in the first place when they were trying to get off cigarettes? Oh wait, most vapers have tried other cessation modalities like NRT only to find them wanting. This does not bode well for vapers if more studies show negative long-term effects.

But this brings us full-circle, to an inescapable part of the puzzle that must be answered— What is the nature of the ecigarette and/or its delivery system that makes it more effective than other nicotine delivery systems?

In general, why are people quitting tobacco smoking at a greater rate by using ecigarettes?

There must be something in the nature of the ecig delivery system that makes it easier for some to quit smoking at better rates than conventional treatments like NRT.

ORALLY FIXATED OR STARVING?

Some will say vaping is more effective in smoking cessation because it is the only method that preserves the act of holding something in your hand while inhaling— and as a bonus, you're getting nicotine with each puff. In other words, the act of vaping not only gives you what you're addicted to (nicotine) but it also retains *vestiges* of the act of smoking cigarettes. Many vapers on internet boards have a name for this nebulous factor— "oral fixation". According to one website which expounds on the matter, the reason smokers eat constantly (a form of oral fixation) when they quit is "because they are subconsciously mimicking the act of smoking, which involves placing something into their mouth." In addition to the nicotine delivery this pretty much sums up the thinking on why vaping is more successful in quitting tobacco.

In reality (as established in chapters 1 thru 3 in addition to chapter

7) the so-called 'oral fixation' is just another term for pica— which, ultimately, is the body's search for silica.

And as we have also shown previously, at one time in the past scientists held a different assumption about pica, or 'oral fixation' if you want to call it that. *They believed that it was due to a nutritional deficiency.* Keep in mind that this was post-Freud also. The psychological explanation for the problem of oral fixation was held at bay until it was 'demonstrated' that the nutrient deficiency explanation was found lacking. Or so it seemed.

Then, to fill the vacuum, the alternative— the 'psychological explanation', which denuded the concept of pica, and which had been floating around in the air for some time, came to fruition as the answer for pica.

It was in the early 1960's that the demolishing of the nutritional deficiency idea began. In the study which accomplished this razing, headed by Margaret Gutelius, it was shown that some children improved their pica (oral fixation) with iron intramuscular administration. At the time it was thought that iron supplementation was the cure for pica. If the pica disappears (as it did with some of the participants in this study) due to a nutrient replacement that's good news, right?

Not so fast. There was also a control group of pica sufferers that had the *same* amount of improvement when they were given an intramuscular saline solution. So that was the end of the idea that a nutrient was the thing that was causing pica or oral fixation. (Nutritional Studies of children with pica, Pediatrics, 29:1012, 1962)

It only took one more influential study to sink the ship of nutritional deficiency as the cause of oral fixation and that was done the following year in 1963.

One group in this study (both groups were suffering from pica) was given a multiple vitamin and mineral solution daily for about six weeks or so. The control group was given a placebo. At the end of the study you can probably guess what happened. Both groups had about the same amount of improvement with their pica problem. (Treatment of Pica with a Vitamin and Mineral Supplement, Am J Clin Nutr. 1963 May;12:388-93)

As mentioned, in the past, scientific efforts were focused on this problem as being nutritional in nature. But now another interpretation was called for and their words bore this out in their conclusion.

"Results of this experiment are in accord with previous findings that pica is a complicated environmental, cultural and psychologic problem." These scientists were really writing a manifesto for the future when it came to researching pica and oral fixation. This was the end of the game for nutrient deficiency as the explanatory cause and the vacuum was soon filled with psychological, Freudian-tinged explanations.

Psychology and psychiatric methods were now the locus of attention for explaining this problem. And so now you have websites and popular literature reciting the same babble.

But the search for the missing nutrient was given up rather hastily by these scientists. It is a distressing fact that the conclusion sounded authoritative, as if all methods and all resources were exhausted in searching for the missing nutrient. We know that was not the case, though, because the scientists themselves wrote in the Gutelius 1962 study, cited above, that "the possibilty remains that some other nutrient or nutrients lacking in the diet might cause pica and thus prove curative in treatment."

And even though they wrote that exclusive sounding conclusion they did admit, earlier in the study, that "It would have been desirable to investigate the treatment of pica with a completely adequate diet or complete nutritional supplement for each child tailored to fit his specific needs. However, from a practical point of view, such procedures were obviously impossible."

Very strange. Why then would you come out with that concluding statement that seemed to exclude the nutrition deficiency angle? Wouldn't you want to reinforce the earlier statement by qualifying the conclusion in reiterating that it's possible that the missing nutrient is still out there and that you just didn't have the time or money to investigate?

The studies did their damage and pica became 'oral fixation' in the psychological sense. Nutrient deficiency as the cause of pica was occluded and the idea slinked off into the background . . . until this book.

VAPERS HAVE FOUND A SOURCE OF SILICA

The central theme of this book is that a cigarette smoker is exhibiting a hunger response by the act of smoking tobacco. This hunger is actually a specific hunger for a nutrient called silica which is contained in the particulate in the tobacco smoke.

Are vapers smoking ecigarettes for the same reason?

Vapers are actually taking in a silica source when they use ecigarettes though in an attenuated form. This is the primary reason why vaping has been somewhat more successful in cessation than other methods. What especially makes it effective is that the silica is in the aerosol, the smoke that comes out of the ecigarette when inhaling. This was found to be the case in a study published in 2013(Metal and Silicate Particles Including Nanoparticles Are Present in Electronic Cigarette Cartomizer Fluid and Aerosol. Monique Williams, PLoS ONE 8(3): e57987).

Besides other elements the authors of the study found "smooth surfaced silicate beads" which they found that "pass through the outer fibers and enter aerosol more readily than the irregularly shaped and heavier tin particles, which were largely trapped among the fibers."

Silica, according to these scientists, is the third most abundant element in the aerosol (see Table 1 of study). The only elements that were in greater amounts in the aerosol were boron and sodium.

The area of the ecigarette that was causing this silica to be in the aerosol, according to these scientists, was in the wick. The wick is one of the main components of every ecigarette— no matter the brand. In other words, you are not going to have an ecigarette without a wick and here's the important part— *every single wick contains silica.*

In general, there are two types of wicks: cotton and silica. Isn't that interesting? Especially if we consider that cotton contains silica. (Role of silicon in developing cotton fibers, Journal of Plant Nutrition, 13:1, 131-148)

Also, the silica wick is the wick of choice for the most popular brand of ecigarette in the United States that teenagers are using. The current national outcry of teens that are becoming "addicted" to ecigs is focused on the nicotine content of course. The reality is that teenagers, because of certain dietary habits which exclude silica, are seeking an alternative silica source— in this case ecigarettes. The angle of attack taken by health authorities is well-intentioned but incorrect. They want to ban access to these products but, as documented in this book, the human body will always find an alternative silica source no matter what. It's a vain enterprise to do such things.

In essence what is happening here is the same story all over again that was documented in the first few chapters— that the human body is fundamentally, above all else, a silica dependent entity. And if silica is witheld from the diet the human body will go on a search mission to obtain it in some other form, even if it's in a nonfood form. (Chapters 1-3 and chapter 7)

In light of the recent "epidemic" of teens smoking ecigarettes, one must remember the following: A child or teenager that is vaping is not addicted to nicotine. They are starving for a specific mineral— and, to a smaller extent, a vitamin.

The same thing applies to all vapers. The problem is specific hunger— not addiction. But it all ends well because there's great news: Since we now know that vaping is due to a specific hunger for silica, all we have to do is feed this hunger via food and/or supplement sources that are high in silica, then the desire to vape will end.

Knowledge converts into power only when that knowledge is incorporated into your very actions. You must *become* the knowledge. If you're vaping you must read all of chapter six and then reread it to come up with your very own action plan. You'll notice the results on the very first day. Smoking will become a historical artifact not only for you but for all of humanity.

Send me your questions and testimonies at the following email address paracelsuspress@gmail.com

The Beginning

One thing I know— I am no Ramanujan. Not even close. If you have read or ever get around to reading *The Man Who Knew Infinity* by Robert Kanigel or even Ken Ono's *My Search For Ramanujan,* you'll discover that Srinivasa Ramanujan, were he alive today, would have more intellect in his pinky finger than you or I have in our brains. Though he died at the age of thirty two, today it's pretty much agreed upon that he was one of the most brilliant mathematicians that ever lived (since many of his theorems have been worked out and proven).

And this leads us another thing that I know— if he appeared today, you would never hire him to teach you or your college age son or daughter anything about mathematics.

Would that be because he would be too difficult to understand? Nope. Maybe his personality would be too coarse? No again. And no to any other objectionable thing you could think of.

You would not accept Ramanujan as your tutor or anyone else's tutor because he has no resume.

You see, Srinivasa Ramanujan had no qualifications.

YOU: Mr. Ramanujan, you say you love mathematics and such but I need a trained, qualified person to train my daughter for her SATs.

RAMANUJAN: Madam, I love mathematics is that not enough? I have self-trained myself with math texts. One text when I was 10 years old until I exhausted every page and exercise in that book and also another math text when I was 16 years old. Plus I have some theorems here that you could look at.

YOU: I don't know anything about theorems and . . . you say you were self-taught? In mathematics? I really need someone who has a piece of paper saying they are qualified to teach my daughter.

RAMANUJAN: Where can I get one of those papers?

Actually, Ramanujan did go to college and failed spectacularly.

All he wanted to do was sit at home and do maths. When the English mathematician GH Hardy met up with Ramanujan he was astounded at how advanced this self-taught fellow was and took him in and introduced him to elite mathematicians. Yet, were he to appear today, he wouldn't be qualified to tutor your child because of no 'words on papers'.

Which brings us to another thing I know a little about— words. Specifically, I'm fascinated by how words change their meaning over time. Take the word 'awful'. It once meant, something that evokes awe, as in, 'God is awful'. Today when you say the word you certainly do not mean that the thing you're talking about is majestic. Or a word like naughty. If someone called someone else 'naughty' a few hundred years ago they were referring to the fact that the other person was destitute, as in being poor, have nothing or, *naught*.

The word *amateur* is rather fascinating. In general, today this word has two shades of meaning and one of them has a rather unflattering sense. An amateur golfer is someone who doesn't get paid. That's one sense. However, another meaning also rides upon that first sense and that is that the person who is an amateur golfer may not be that good— or at least as good as someone who gets paid to play golf. And that secondary meaning can be magnified into a derogatory sense as in, "Those plumbers did an amateur job."

But the original sense of the word *amateur* had a much different meaning. As late as the 1860s we see a usage far different from what it is today. In a travel book entitled Recollections of the Tartar Steppes (1863) the author, one Mrs Atkinson, uses the word amateur in a completely alien sense to our ears. Here's an example: "I am no amateur of these melons." Let me translate what she was actually saying: "I am no *lover* of these melons." The first definition in the Oxford English Dictionary for amateur was, and still is, "someone who loves or is fond of something". An amateur is a lover. It comes from the Latin by way of the French language. The Latin verb amare means "to love".

The second meaning in the Oxford states that an amateur is "one who cultivates anything as a pastime" rather than for pay as a professional.

So it's a fascinating scenario today when plumbers (or anyone else for that matter) who do shoddy work are called 'amateurs'. Do we mean that they are *lovers* of plumbing? Probably not. Strange change though, huh? The professional plumber has his papers with words saying that he is qualified. In the older usage, does that make him an amateur (lover) of plumbing? Not necessarily. But in the modern usage, though he has words on papers (licenses and such), he can be still considered an amateur!

Do you see what's going on here?

Does anyone really think that an 'amateur', in the original sense, could do shoddy work? I rather think that an amateur, a lover, would be near the top of their field and do exquisite work. This type of person is who I would want making my burger or doing work on my house or anything else in between— I would want a lover rather than words on a paper.

A lover could only bring good results. Practical results.

Which brings us to another thing that you and I know very well— utility. This is the big idea behind this brief excursus. What really undergirds this whole discussion is the little thing that permeates every area of our existence— pragmatism. We live in a civilization that, above everything else, honors results. We're permitted little games, and such, where we put words on papers and stamp cards and hand out certificates but the fact of the matter is we don't care where an answer to a problem comes from as long as it works. We'll gladly overlook "words on papers' if the job gets done. I know this and you know this.

Yet here we are in a civilization that pushes 'words on papers'. This is all well and good, I suppose, if that certification brings about an outcome that 'works', that solves the problem at hand. But there's a rather odd scenario that mitigates against this, that tells a different story. And it's right there in front of our noses. At no other time in human history have we had more people who have "words on papers". And there are a good many that have extra, extra "words on papers". These the world calls 'experts' and 'professionals'. So, though our civilization and its institutions strive to bring about "professionalization" of services and skills (words on papers), a strange irony has resulted from this: Though the world is seemingly blessed with all these people and all these experts with "words on papers", the world has never had more problems than at any other time in its history. In the very same fields that we have the proliferation of the experts and professionals.

Have you ever thought this odd?

It would take a book to document and analyze this phenomenon. Thankfully the philosopher Ivan Illich made this a lifelong pursuit and we have the riches of his research in several books. Two of his targets were the fields of education (*Deschooling Society* 1971) and health (*Medical Nemesis: The Expropriation of Health* 1975) in which he demonstrates that whenever professionalization becomes dominant in a field, there will eventually be more problems in that field than before.

For example, everyone is familiar with the problems that have plagued the field of education for some time. But this denigration occurred just after the field was infused with great amounts of money and hence, professionalization. With the coming of the 'experts' the problem got worse.

But there's more, there is much more to this phenomenon that Illich explicates so well.

One of the disturbing outcomes that Illich talks about is that professionalization is forever in search of, as he calls it, the "professional client". A client for life. To accomplish this calls for a creative act on behalf of the profession. To keep a client forever means that the "problem" would have to be seen as an enduring one or that new problems would have to be created as offshoots to the original problem. In the case of an enduring problem we see that psychoanalysis may claim individuals for the term of their life. You can never be 'fixed', so to speak, in one session or one hundred or one thousand. No one really knows. But if a true cause was ever to be found, leading to cure, the profession would cease to exist.

As to the creation of new problems Illich cites the medical field. One of the techniques is 'moving goalposts'. For example, at one time there was such a thing as a patient being diabetic and everyone knew what that was. Now there is such a thing as being "pre-diabetic". Logically one could say that everyone is prediabetic. Illich claims that the latter technique, creating a new problem out of the old one, is the usual road taken in order to spread the net further, encompassing more and more people to become clients. But if there is always a new problem stemming from an old one, and a newer problem stemming from the 'new problem', one can barely fix their sight on solving the original problem because now there is layer upon layer encrusted and no one wants to go back to the point of origin— the original problem. In other words, the nature of professionalization may be the exact opposite of what it presents itself to be. According to Illich, getting 'words on papers' may actually be a device to not only monopolize knowledge as much as to stunt it, even to prevent it.

THE CRUX

This is all just to say that I am very much like Ramanujan— in the sense that I am an autodidact. That is to say, an autodidact with the same level of passion as he.

His passion was math and he reached a very high-level of accomplishment through books or texts.

This can only be done through love of the subject matter. However, some autodidacts have more than one.

When one has several "loves", a rather fascinating thing begins to happen over a period of time. Seepage. Slowly but surely the principles of one subject matter begin to "leak through" or interpenetrate into another field of interest and a strange hybrid of thinking begins to overcome the mind. This takes time and deep study, however, before one begins to notice it.

As shown in chapter eight, there was a cross-contamination, a seepage, between a couple fields of knowledge that proved very helpful. In reality it solved the cigarette smoking problem once and for all. The only reason that happened was because of my deep interests in those varying fields. Because I certainly was not looking for an answer to the smoking problem.

That only happened as a result of serendipity . . . Well, of course.

But the catalyst was love.

www.ingramcontent.com/pod-product-compliance
Lightning Source LLC
Chambersburg PA
CBHW032224080426
42735CB00008B/708